Clifford Richardson

Third report on the chemical composition and physical properties of American cereals,

Wheat, oats, barley and rye

Clifford Richardson

Third report on the chemical composition and physical properties of American cereals,
Wheat, oats, barley and rye

ISBN/EAN: 9783337732936

Printed in Europe, USA, Canada, Australia, Japan

Cover: Foto ©ninafisch / pixelio.de

More available books at **www.hansebooks.com**

DEPARTMENT OF AGRICULTURE,
DIVISION OF CHEMISTRY.

BULLETIN   **No. 9.**

THIRD REPORT

ON THE

CHEMICAL COMPOSITION AND PHYSICAL PROPERTIES

OF

AMERICAN CEREALS,

WHEAT, OATS, BARLEY, AND RYE.

BY

CLIFFORD RICHARDSON.

WASHINGTON:
GOVERNMENT PRINTING OFFICE.
1886.

13734—No. 9

LETTERS OF TRANSMITTAL.

I.

UNITED STATES DEPARTMENT OF AGRICULTURE,
DIVISION OF CHEMISTRY,
Washington, D. C., April 2, 1886.

SIR: I have the honor to submit herewith for your approval the final results of the investigations of American cereals which have been made by this Division under the direction of Mr. Clifford Richardson. These investigations, it is believed, are the most extensive and thorough of any similar ones heretofore carried on, and have revealed the influence of soil and climate on the composition of our grain in a manner which will prove beneficial both to our farmers and manufacturers.

Respectfully,

H. W. WILEY,
Chemist.

Hon. N. J. COLMAN,
Commissioner.

II.

MARCH 31, 1886.

SIR: I have the honor to hand you for transmission to the Commissioner of Agriculture my third report upon American cereals.

Very respectfully,

CLIFFORD RICHARDSON,
Assistant Chemist.

Dr. H. W. WILEY,
Chemist.

COMPOSITION AND PROPERTIES OF AMERICAN CEREALS.

WHEAT.

In previous reports, Bulletins 1 and 4 of the Chemical Division, we have discussed the changes in composition of many varieties of wheat as they have been grown in Colorado during a period of years by Prof. A. E. Blount. His attempts have been to improve by selection and crossing the character of this grain both for the farmer and miller. What success he has met with in increasing the yield and physical characteristics will be evident from the data which follow. It has been our province to study the changes in the chemical composition of the grain from year to year, showing the result of varying conditions in this direction. This has been done for four years, and before giving the results of the last year's examination a summary of those of previous years will serve to make them more intelligible.

The first specimens of wheat were handed to the Division by Professor Blount in 1881, and were of varieties which had been grown two and three years in Colorado. They numbered thirty-three, and had the following average composition:

Weight of 100 grains.	Grams 4.865.
Water ....per cent..	9.86
Ash..............................do ...	2.28
Oil........ ....do....	2.41
Carbohydrates ....do....	70.48
Crude fiber ....do....	1.57
Albuminoids.....................do....	13.40
Total......	100.00
Nitrogen.......................do....	2.14

From this average it was learned that in that year Colorado produced a grain very rich in albuminoids, large in size, dry, and with little fiber or hull.

Among the specimens it was found that some were from domestic and others from foreign seed, part being Russian. Knowing that Russian wheat is the richest in albuminoids of any in the world, and that continental varieties as a rule contain more than our own, it was of interest to observe that the crops grown in Colorado were still characterized by the source of the seed.

Average composition of crops from seed from various sources.

	Domestic seed.	Foreign seed.	Russian seed.
Weight of 100 grains ....grams..	4.714	5.187	5.075
Water ....per cent..	9.85	9.86	9.69
Ash ....do....	2.27	2.32	2.41
Oil ....do....	2.38	2.45	2.44
Carbhydrates ....do....	70.87	69.46	69.33
Crude fiber ....do....	1.58	1.57	1.59
Albuminoids ....do....	13.05	14.34	14.54
Total	100.00	100.00	100.00
Nitrogen ....per cent..	2.09	2.29	2.32

These wheats were the richest in albuminoids of any that had been examined up to that time in this country. Since then the hard spring wheats of the Northwest have been found to be more nitrogenous, but not comparable in their size or yield.

The second year, twelve varieties, grown from seed supplied by the Department of Agriculture, were analyzed. After one year, that is to say, the first year's growth in Colorado, they were found to have all increased in size, and instead of an average weight of 3.402 grams per hundred grains, they weighed 4.299 grams. As regards the percentage of albuminoids, where the seed wheat was low in nitrogen there was a gain, but as half of the varieties contained originally more albuminoids than the average Colorado grain, there was a drop in six of the twelve specimens toward the average. For example, a seed having 16.11 per cent. of albuminoids, the crop fell to 14.91 per cent., while one having only 9.65 rose to 12.15 per cent. From these facts, and the analyses of the previous year, the conclusion was drawn that the conditions in Colorado were suited to the production of a grain containing about 13 per cent. of albuminoids.

This was undoubtedly the case at the time. In the two following years, however, these conditions have been somewhat modified.

In the third year, 57 varieties were examined, 28 of which had been analyzed before in 1881. A loss of albuminoids occurred in all but 4 cases, and a loss of weight in all. The average for the year was—

Weight of 100 grains.	Grams 3.941.
Water ....per cent..	9.38
Ash ....do....	2.09
Oil, carbhydrates, and crude fiber...do...	76.79
Albuminoids ....do....	11.74
Total............................	100.00
Nitrogen ....per cent..	1.88

This sudden change and drop in size and percentage of albuminoids were attributed by Professor Blount to a heavy hail-storm, which prostrated the crop in its formation stage and influenced all its characteristics. This was probably the case, and it became of great interest to study the crop of 1884, to learn what the recovery might be, and what, after from one to six years' growth in Colorado, the changes in average composition might amount to.

To this end 77 varieties, selected from a lot of 200 grown by Professor Blount, have been examined chemically and physically, and the results are presented in the following tables, together with certain data in regard to yield per acre, as well as characteristics of the seasons and other conditions, taken from Professor Blount's report and personal letters.

Names, sources of seed, yield, &c., of Colorado wheats.

No.	Name of wheat.	Seed received from—	Color.		Bearded or smooth.	Yield per square rod, pounds.						Bushels per acre, 1884.
			Grain.	Chaff.		1879.	1880.	1881.	1882.	1883.	1884.	
1	Minnesota Fife	Minnesota	White	White	Smooth	6	7	10	19	7½	16½	44
2	White Fife	do	do	do	do	7	7	11	15½	8	15	40
3	Sherman	Pennsylvania	Amber	Red	Bearded	6	7½	9	18	8	17	45⅓
4	White Russian	Moscow	do	White	Smooth	5	8	14	14½	7	21	56
5	Odessa	Black Sea	Red	Red	do	6	7½	14	13	8	18	48
6	Eldorado	California	White	White	Bearded	4½	5	16	17	9	20	53⅓
7	Soft Australian	Australia	do	do	Smooth	4¾	9½	17	14½	11	20	53⅓
8	Defiance	Vermont	do	do	do	5¾	8½	15	17½	7	22	58⅔
9	Champlain	do	do	do	Bearded	5¾	7	11	18	8	22	58⅔
10	Oregon Club	Oregon	do	do	Smooth	6½	7	15	17¾	11	19	50⅔
11	Australian Hard	Australia	do	do	do	8¾	8½	16	16	8	19½	52
12	Sonora	Mexico	do	Red	do	5	6½	14	16½	5	21	56
13	White Mexican	Siberia	do	White	do	6¼	8½	13	14½	5	15½	41⅓
14	Improved Fife	Minnesota	do	do	do	5	5½	13	17	8	21	56
15	Russian	Russia	Amber	do	do	5	5½	14	19	8	19½	52
16	Brooks	Pennsylvania	White	do	do	4½	5½	16	15	7	19	50⅔
17	Rio Grande	Mexico	Red	do	Bearded	5	10	11	17	12	21	56
18	Canada Club	Canada	White	do	Smooth	5½	6	11	19	6	19	50⅔
19	Judkin	Pennsylvania	do	do	do	6½	5	10	18	6	20	53⅓
20	Lost Nation	Illinois	Red	do	do	5½	4½	11	17	6	15½	41⅓
21	Touzelle	France	White	do	Bearded	6	5	15	18	4	17	45⅓
22	Australian Club	Australia	do	do	Smooth	7	6	13	19½	6	19	50⅔
23	Golden Globe	Pennsylvania	do	do	Bearded	5½	4	9	15½	7	17½	48⅔
24	Mediterranean Spring	Italy	Amber	do	do	6	5	10	14	9	19	50⅔
25	China Tea	Pekin	do	do	do	5	4½	12	18	7	21	56
26	Chili	Chili	White	do	Smooth	6½	5½	9	19½	9	17	45⅓
27	China Spring	Pekin	Amber	do	do	6	6	14	18	10	22	58⅔
28	Egyptian	Egypt	White	do	Bearded	6½	6	15	15¾	10	18	48
29	Saxon Fife	Germany	Amber	do	Smooth	6½	5½	12	19½	6	24	64
30	Dominion	Virginia	do	Red	do	5	5	13	19	12	25	66⅔
31	Prussian	Prussia	White	White	do	5½	4½	14	14	10	19	50⅔
32	Golden Drop	Iowa	do	do	do	4½	6	14	17½	10	20	53⅓
33	Pringle's No. 6	Vermont	do	do	do	5	4¾	10	19	5½	21	56
34	Pringle's No. 4	do	do	do	do	5½	6	15	17	6	17	45⅓
35	Pringle's No. 5	do	do	do	do	6	7	10	19	7	23	61⅓
36	Winter Australian	Australia	do	do	do	7	8	11	17½	8	19	50⅔
37	Clawson	Pennsylvania	White	Red	do	4½	8	17	24	11	29	77⅓
38	Fultz	do	Red	White	do	4½	6½	15	23	13	31	82⅔
39	Midge Proof	Wisconsin	White	do	do	4½	5	6	14	6	23	61⅓
40	Black Centennial	New South Wales	do	do	Bearded	5	9	10	25	3	24	64

41	Hedgerow	Egypt	do	do	Smooth	4	7½	6	17	5	18	48
42	Blount's No. 9	(Made here)	do	do	do	3	8	8	19½	7	20	53⅓
43	Italian	Italy	do	do	Bearded	4	5	9	15	8	17	45⅓
44	New York Flint	Genesee	do	do	Smooth	5½	7½	6	17½	6	19	50
45	Bald Baltic	Berlin	do	do	do	6	4½	8	14	8	16½	44
46	Illinois First Premium	Illinois	Amber			4	8½	8	17	6	18	48
47	Illinois Second Premium	do	do		Smooth	4	7	9	18½	2½	25	66⅔
48	Red Orange	do	Red			6	7½	14	19	11	21	56
49	Mediterranean Winter	France				5	6	7	17	7	18	48
50	Turkey	England				6½	5	8	16	9	17	45⅓
51	Blount's No. 10	(Made here)			Smooth		11	14	25½	8	23	61⅓
52	Golden Chaff	Iowa					4	9	17	6	18	48
53	Red Chaff Mediterranean	do					7	8	15	7	16	42⅔
54	Velvet Chaff	do	Red		Smooth		5½	6	16	8	19	50⅔
55	Turkey	Adrianople			do		7	8	18	8	18	48
56	Blount's No. 13	(Made here)			do		8	9	17	7	17	45⅓
57	Blount's No. 15	do			Bearded		7	8	14½	8	21	56
58	Blount's No. 16	do			Smooth		6½	5	19	7	15	40
59	Blount's No. 17	do			Bearded		7	7	20	8	21	56
60	Blount's No. 18	do			do		9	7	18½	6	21	56
61	Blount's No. 19	do			Smooth		7½	14	20½	6	18	48
62	Blount's No. 21	do			Bearded		8	4	19	7	16	42⅔
63	Black Chaff	Hungary			do		4½	5	15	8	17	45⅓
64	Cretan	Crete	White		do		5	3	14	5	20	53⅓
65	Andriola Red	Italy	Red		do		6	8	18	7	21	56
66	Andriola Amber	do	do		do		7	21	20	11	23	61⅓
67	Purple Chaff	Spain	do		do		6½	3	16	3	24	64
68	Boughton	Virginia	White		Smooth		7	1	20½	6	18	48
69	Hedgerow	Leipzig	do		do		6	14	17	8	21	56
70	Anantka	Poland	do		Bearded		5½	5	16	4	15	40
71	Fountain	Montana	do		Smooth		7	13	24	8	20	53⅓
72	Palestine	Palestine	Red		do		7	6	23	9	15	40
73	White Chaff	S. O.	do		do		5½	18	14	8	20	53
74	do	B. O.	do		Bearded		6	13	15	8	15	40
75	Red Chaff	do	do		do		5	15	14	9	15	40
76	Perfection	New York	White		Smooth			6	22	7	13	34⅔
77	German Fife	Berlin	Red		Bearded			7	23	7	21	56
78	Mammoth	do	White		Smooth			9	21½	9	19	50⅔
79	Triticum	St. Petersburg	do		Bearded			12	14	10	17	45⅓
80	Samara	Saratow	Amber		do			6	18	6	19	50⅔
81	Durum	Amoor	White		do			3	17	5	18	48
82	Saratow	Saratow	Red		do			12	10½	9	17⅛	40⅔
83	Ames	Moscow	Amber		do			7	16	9	18	48
84	Moscow	do	Red		do			6	17	5	15	40
85	Knap	Urals	do		Smooth			8	19½	10	17½	46⅔
86	Scotch Fife	Scotland	do		do			8	20	6½	17½	46⅔
87	Doty	Volga	do		Bearded			10	18	11	21	56
88	Meekius	Azor	do		do			7	21	10	22	58⅔
89	White Michigan	Michigan	do		Smooth			2	19½	6	20	53⅓
90	Rickenbrode	Pennsylvania			do			17	19	11	24	64
91	Red Siberian	Siberia	Red					19	20	10	21	56

Names, sources of seed, yield, &c., of Colorado wheat—Continued.

No.	Name of wheat.	Seed received from—	Color.		Bearded or smooth.	Yield per square rod, pounds.						Bushels per acre, 1884.
			Grain.	Chaff.		1879.	1880.	1881.	1882.	1883.	1884.	
92	Heige's Prolific	Pennsylvania	Amber		Smooth			14	22	12	24	64
93	Blue Beard	Black Sea	do					3	18	20	22	58⅔
94	Rice	Maryland			Smooth				12	12	17½	46⅔
95	Swamp	Tennessee			Bearded				9	8	24½	65⅓
96	Gold Medal	Canada			Smooth				11	13	24	64
97	Glass	Pennsylvania			do				12	11	27	72
98	German Amber	Germany			do				11	10	23	61⅓
99	Wysor	Virginia			do				9	7	18	48
100	Dallas	Texas			do				8	13	17½	46⅔
101	Champion Amber	Pennsylvania			do				7	11	21	56
102	Finlay	Canada			do				10	10	23	61⅓
103	Lemon	Pennsylvania			do				8½	9	24	64
104	McGee's Red	Virginia			Bearded				9	8	15	40
105	Bennett	West Virginia			do.				11	11	29	77⅓
106	Early May	Alabama	Red						8	8	16	42⅔
107	Rocky Mountain	California							6	7	17	45⅓
108	Silver Chaff	Kansas							7½	9	18	48
109	Blue Stem	Pennsylvania	White						9	4	18½	52⅔
110	Propos	California	do		Smooth				7	7	21	56
111	Small Frame	Kansas							5	9	17	45⅓
112	Red Clawson	Virginia			Smooth				6	9	22	58⅔
113	Yellow Missouri	Missouri							3	11	18	48
114	Walker	Georgia	Red						8	10	13	34⅔
115	Utah	Salt Lake	White						6	2	17	45⅓
116	Zimmerman	Ohio	Red						8	7	19	50⅔
117	Big May	do			Smooth				7	10	21	56
118	Blount's No. 22	(Made here)							6	3	18	48
119	Blount's No. 23	do			Smooth				7	4	21	56
120	Blount's No. 24	do			do				7	2	22	58⅔
121	Blount's No. 25	do			do				8	4	19	50⅔
122	Blount's No. 26	do			do				7	4	22	58⅔
123	Blount's No. 27	do			do				9	2	19	50⅔
124	Blount's No. 28	do			do				8	3	23	61⅓
125	Blount's No. 29	do			do				7	3	17	45⅓
126	Blount's No. 30	do			do				8	3	19	50⅔
127	Blount's No. 31	do							7	3	18	48
128	Blount's No. 32	do							9	2	20	53⅓
129	Blount's No. 33	do			Smooth				10	3	17	45⅓
130	Blount's No. 34	do			Bearded				5	2	15	40
131	Casaca	Spain			do				8	1	16	42⅔

132	Califat	New Zealand			8	3	17½	46⅔
133	Tuscan	do			7	4	15	40
134	Essex	do			9	3	13	34⅔
135	Tuskana	do			8	3	16½	44
136	Pearl	do			7	4	18	48
137	Hunter's	do			6	4	16	50⅔
138	W. C. Red	Pennsylvania			7	6	16	42⅔
139	Square-head Essex	England			8	2	13	34⅔
140	Gold Drop	do			7	1	15	40
141	Blue Chaff	do			6	2	13	34⅔
142	Chiddum	do			5	2	15	40
143	Venice	Italy			4	4	13½	36
144	Apennine	do			4	3	17	45⅓
145	R. Oregon Club	Oregon		Bearded	5	6	17½	46⅔
146	Hedgerow	do		Smooth	8	3	17	45⅓
147	Aowse	Montana	White	do	8	5	22	58⅔
148	Monmouth	Illinois		Bearded	6	5	18	48
149	Russian Spring	Winnipeg	Red	Smooth	7	7	20	53⅓
150	Vermilion	do		do	8	3	17½	46⅔
151	Smoky	do	Red	Bearded	9	4	20	53⅓
152	Edenton Fife	do	do	Smooth	5	6	18	48
153	Nox No. 2	Vermont	White	do	3	3½	17½	46⅔
154	Nox No. 1	do	do	do	7	6	17	45⅓
155	Nox No. 4	do	Red	Bearded	6	3	21	56
156	Nox No. 3	do	Amber	do	8	2	15	40
157	Nox No. 5	do	White	Smooth	7	4½	18	48
158	Pringle's No. 17	do	do	do	5½	5	17	45⅓
159	Pringle's No. 26	do	do	do	9	2	16	42⅔
160	Wales	New South Wales	Amber	do	8	4	18	48
161	Dead Sea	Palestine			7	3	17	45⅓
162	Northcote's Improved	Washington Territory	White	Smooth	8	5	15	40
163	Northcote's Amber	do	Amber	do	6	5	16½	44
164	White May	Alabama				1	13	34⅔
165	Cat Mountain	California	Red			3	15	40
166	Reed Straw	Ohio				1	14	37⅓
167	Cayahuga	New York				1	13	34⅔
168	Black Chaff	Russia	Red	Smooth		1	16	42⅔
169	Blount's No. 35	(Made here)		do		1	17	45⅓
170	Velvet Amber	Ohio				1	15	40
171	Hebron	Jerusalem	Amber			7	19	50⅔
172	Blount's No. 30	(Made here)				1	10	42⅔
173	White Mediterranean	France	White	Smooth		7	18	48
174	Red Mediterranean	do	Red			6	17	45⅓
175	French Imperial	do	do	do		7	24	64
176	Nebraska	Nebraska	White	Bearded		3	17	45⅓
177	White	North Carolina	do	Smooth		1	20	53⅓
178	Kivet	do	Amber	do		5	26	69⅓
179	Rust Proof	do	Red	do		6	20	53⅓
180	Baltimore	do	White	do		2	18	48
181	Davis	do	Red	do		3	32	85⅓
182	Purple Straw	do	do	do		7	27	72

Names, sources of seed, yield, &c., of Colorado wheats—Continued.

No.	Name of wheat.	Seed received from—	Color.		Bearded or smooth.	Yield per square rod, pounds.						Bushels per acre, 1884.
			Grain.	Chaff.		1879.	1880.	1881.	1882.	1883.	1884.	
183	Gold Premium	North Carolina	White		Smooth					4	32½	86⅔
184	Hick's Prolific	do	Red		do					3	20	53⅓
185	Earnhart	do	White		do					2½	22	58⅔
186	Wintergreen	do	do		do					2	21	56
187	St. Leger	Scotland								1	18	48
188	Cheshire	do								1	15	40
189	Hunter	do								2	17	45⅓
190	Oakshotts	do								1	18	48
191	Hardwick	do								3	19	50⅔
192	Geiger	Divide	White		Smooth					5	16	42⅔
193	Blount's No. 37	(Made here)								6	17½	46⅔
194	Sea Island	Washington			Bearded					1	17	45⅓
195	Edenton	Winnepeg			do					2	15	40
196	Winnepeg Russian	do	Red		Smooth					2	15⅝	41⅔
197	Manitoba	do	do		Bearded					2	15	40
198	Winnepeg	do	Amber		do					1	15	40
199	Russia Winnepeg	do	Red		Smooth					3	16	42⅔
200	Hallet's Pedigree	England	White		do					2	17	45⅓
201	Sibley's No. 1	Rochester			Bearded					2	14	37⅓
202	French Black Chaff	France			do					2	15	40
203	Rural	New York			do						12	32
204	Velvet Club	Germany									10	26⅔
205	Austrian	Austria									9	23
206	Bohemian	Bohemia									7	19⅓
207	Whittington	California									10	26⅔
208	Snow Flake	do			Smooth						9	23
209	Beardless Velvet	do									8	21⅓
210	Taganrog	do									7	19⅔
211	Michigan Amber	Michigan	Red								11	29⅓
212	China No. 1	Pekin			Bearded						8	21⅓
213	China No. 2	do									9	23
214	Missouri Turkey	Missouri			Bearded						7	19⅔
215	Missouri Mediterranean	do			do						11	29⅓
216	California Walker	California			do						9	23
217	Ohio White	Ohio									13	34⅔
218	India Red	India									10	26⅔
219	Andrus Black	New York									7	19⅔
220	Mediterranean Hybrid	do									11	29⅓
221	Andrus Flint	do									6	16
222	Scottish Fife	Washington			Smooth						12	32

ye	Hungary		8
rankenstein	Germany		7
larch	California	do	11
landers	Flanders	do	12
lourelle	France		9
ictoria	England		8
ircassian	Circassia		11
V. Velvet	Ireland		14

Of his method of cultivation Professor Blount says:

It is quite simple. I sow only one ounce of picked seed per square rod in eight rows, or in field culture only thirty pounds per acre. On each square rod I put home-made fertilizers, horse, cow, hog, and sheep manure, the latter being by far the best in this climate. In the case of cow and hog manures, one cubic foot is used, but two cubic feet of horse manure. There are also plots with no manures. My crops are hoed twice and irrigated twice.

Of the seasons he says:

1879 was a fair wheat year, no rain from April to harvest; 1880 two showers, doing more damage to wheat than none; 1881 and 1882 fair wheat seasons; 1883 hail killed everything, and 1884 a fine season with some rain.

A description of his methods of crossing and selection will be found in the Annual Report of this Department for 1881–'82, and in the report of the agricultural department of the Colorado State College for 1884.

In addition it is necessary to say that it must be borne in mind that these wheats have been grown upon an experimental scale and with greater care and regularity of condition than could be often found in field culture in this country. While they do not represent, therefore, the ordinary product of the State from which they come, they are more valuable for purposes of scientific comparison and as a guide to what may be done by the farmer in the improvement of his seed and crops.

Physical properties of Colorado wheat, 1884.

Name.	Collection number.	Serial number.	Color.	Bearded or smooth.	Yield per acre.	Weight per bushel.	Weight per 100 grains.	Years in cultivation.
					Bus.	*Lbs.*	*Grains.*	
Oregon Club	10	3500	Light amber	S.	50⅔	63.7	3.647	6
Australian Hard	11	3501	....do	S.	52	......	4.041	6
Sonora	12	3502	Yellow	S.	56	67.3	3.830	6
White Mexican	13	3503	....do	S.	41⅓	63.5	4.890	6
Improved Fife	14	3504	Light amber	S.	56	65.8	3.672	6
Brooks	16	3505	Amber	S.	50⅔	65.0	3.841	6
Rio Grande	17	3506	..do	B.	56	67.1	4.743	6
Canada Club	18	3507	....do	S.	50⅔	66.1	3.764	6
Judkin	19	3508	Dark amber	S.	53⅓	64.1	3.920	6
Lost Nation	20	3509	Amber	S.	41⅓	64.5	4.147	6
Touzelle	21	3510	Lighter amber	B.	45⅓	65.7	4.300	6
Australian Club	22	3511	Amber white	S.	50⅔	64.8	4.536	6
Golden Globe	23	3512	Amber	B.	48⅔	66.5	4.670	6
Mediterranean Spring	24	3513	....do	B.	50⅔	66.2	4.640	6
China Tea	25	3514	do	B.	56	67.0	5.000	6
Chili	26	3515	Yellow	S.	45⅓	64.9	4.440	6
China Spring	27	3516	Dark amber	S.	58⅔	65.4	3.990	6
Egyptian Fife	28	3517	Yellow amber	B.	48	63.8	4.840	6
Saxon Fife	29	3518	Red	S.	64	65.3	3.690	6
Danubian	30	3519	Red and yellow	S.	66⅔	62.5	4.110	6
Prussian	31	3520	Dark amber	S.	50⅔	64.0	3.610	6
Pringle	34	3521	Light amber	S.	45⅓	......	4.300	6
Hedge Row, White Chaff	41	3522	Yellow amber	S.	48	65.9	3.170	6
Italian	43	3523	Red and yellow	B.	45⅓	64.1	5.620	6
Hybrid No. 10	51	3524	Pale yellow	S.	61⅓	63.9	4.690	5
Nox No. 1	54	3525	Yellow and amber	S.	50⅔	64.8	3.080	5
Hybrid No. 13	56	3526	Amber	S.	45⅛	62.7	3.160	5
Hybrid No. 15	57	3527	Yellow and amber	B.	56	63.6	3.200	5
Hybrid No. 16	58	3528	Red and amber	S.	40	62.8	4.110	5
Hybrid No. 17	59	3529	Red	B.	56	66.8	4.740	5

Physical properties of Colorado wheat, 1884—Continued.

Name.	Collection number.	Serial number.	Color.	Bearded or smooth.	Yield per acre.	Weight per bushel.	Weight per 100 grains.	Years in cultivation.
					Bus.	*Lbs.*	*Grains.*	
Andriola Amber	66	3530	Red and amber	B.	61⅓	66.4	3.790	5
Red Clawson	112	3531	Dark amber	S.	58⅔	66.0	3.660	3
Big Mary	117	3532	Dark yellow	S.	56	63.5	4.710	3
Hybrid No. 26	122	3533	Light amber	S.	58⅔	65.9	5.339	3
Hybrid No. 28	124	3534	Dark yellow	S.	61⅛	62.2	4.683	3
Hybrid No. 33	129	3535	do	S.	45⅓	62.8	3.586	3
Hybrid No. 34	130	3536	Glassy amber	B.	40	64.4	6.620	3
Casaca	131	3537	Red	B.	42⅔	....	3.299	3
Monmouth	148	3538	Light red	B.	48	67.0	4.830	3
Russian Spring	149	3539	Red	S.	53⅓	64.3	3.880	3
Vermillion	150	3540	do	S.	46⅔	64.9	3.500	3
Edenton Fife	152	3541	do	S.	48	63.5	4.100	3
Nox 2	153	3542	Yellow amber	S.	46⅔	65.7	4.170	3
Nox 4	155	3543	Light red	B.	56	66.1	4.670	3
Nox 3	156	3544	Glassy amber	B.	40	67.2	5.505	3
Nox 5	157	3545	Yellow amber	S.	48	65.0	4.239	3
Pringle No. 17	158	3546	do	S.	45⅔	64.2	4.167	3
Wiles	160	3547	Light amber	S.	48	64.6	5.073	3
Northcote's Imperial	162	3548	Yellow	S.	40	63.7	3.576	3
Northcote's Amber	163	3549	Light red	S.	44	64.1	4.120	3
Black Chaff	168	3550	Red	S.	42⅔	66.7	3.420	2
Hybrid No. 35	169	3551	Amber yellow	S.	45⅔	62.2	3.800	2
Hebron	171	3552	do	......	50⅔	63.9	3.500	2
Mediterranean White	173	3553	Deep yellow	S.	48	66.9	3.580	2
French Imperial	175	3554	Red	S.	64	66.6	4.880	2
Nebraska	176	3555	Amber	B.	45⅔	66.4	4.440	2
Northcote's White	177	3556	Light amber	S.	53⅓	64.6	4.400	2
Kivet	178	3557	Deep yellow	S.	69⅓	65.0	4.220	2
Baltimore	180	3558	Light red	S.	48	67.1	5.060	2
Davis	181	3559	do	S.	85⅓	66.1	4.220	2
Gold Premium	183	3560	do	S.	66⅔	65.7	4.120	2
Hick's Prolific	184	3561	Red	S.	53⅓	66.1	3.890	2
Wintergreen	186	3562	Amber	S.	56	66.9	3.930	2
Geiger	192	3563	do	S.	42	......	4.240	2
Hybrid No. 37	193	3564	Amber yellow	......	46⅔	64.2	3.850	2
Sea Island	194	3565	Red	B.	45⅔	......	3.420	2
Edenton	195	3566	Amber	B.	40	65.6	5.180	2
Winnipeg, Russian	196	3567	Light red	S.	41⅔	64.4	4.120	2
Manitoba	197	3568	Red	B.	40	66.3	3.580	2
Winnipeg	198	3569	Glassy amber	B	40	67.8	5.560	2
Hallett's Pedigree	200	3570	Amber and yellow	S.	45⅔	64.5	3.880	2
China No. 2	213	3571	Amber	......	24	67.7	3.180	1
Mo. Turkey	214	3572	do	B.	18⅔	......	4.000	1
Mo. Mediterranean	215	3573	Light red	B.	29⅓	......	4.480	1
Scotch Fife	222	3574	Red	S.	32	64.6	3.440	1
Rye	223	3575	Dark and light red	S.	21⅓	64.7	4.760	1
Sandomirka	233	3576	Dark red	......	......	68.6	4.060	1
Hopetown	235	3577	Amber	......	......	67.0	4.500	1

Analyses of Colorado wheat, 1874.

Name.	Collection number.	Serial number.	Color.	Weight of 100 grams. Grams.	Water. Pr. ct.	Ash. Pr. ct.	Oil. Pr. ct.	Carbohy-drates. Pr. ct.	Fiber. Pr. ct.	Albumin-oids. Pr. ct.	Nitrogen. Pr. ct.	Season of growth.	Gluten. Moist.	Gluten. Dry.	Quality of gluten.
Oregon Club	10	3500	Light amber	3.647	6.93	1.98	2.13	75.58	2.18	11.20	1.79	6	23.75	8.71	
Australian Hard	11	3501	do	4.041	7.40	2.05	1.95	74.76	2.05	11.73	1.88	6	32.20	11.81	
Sonora	12	3502	Yellow	3.830	7.31	1.90	2.27	74.64	1.63	12.25	1.96	6	36.18	13.37	
White Mexican	13	3503	do	4.580	7.27	2.05	1.94	75.09	1.50	11.55	1.85	6	35.01	12.70	
Improved Fife	14	3504	Light amber	3.672	8.72	1.78	2.21	71.18	1.90	14.16	2.27	6	45.12	16.16	
Brooks	16	3505	Amber	3.841	6.68	1.80	1.96	74.55	1.88	13.13	2.10	6	38.72	13.70	
Rio Grande	17	3506	do	4.743	8.74	1.52	2.49	72.92	1.99	12.43	1.99	6	32.83	11.76	
Canada Club	18	3507	do	3.764	7.85	1.87	2.14	74.11	1.90	12.13	1.96	6	28.65	10.80	
Judkin	19	3508	Dark amber	3.920	7.63	1.94	2.02	74.06	1.85	12.43	1.99	6	30.45	11.28	
Lost Nation	20	3509	Amber	4.147	7.29	1.53	2.25	74.06	1.60	12.08	1.93	6	27.70	10.12	
Touzelle	21	3510	Light amber	4.300	6.98	1.79	1.94	73.51	1.48	14.18	2.27	6	44.64	14.88	
Australian Club	22	3511	Mixed amber and white	4.536	7.16	1.16	1.98	75.40	1.45	12.08	1.93	6	27.49	9.39	
Golden Globe	24	3512	Amber	4.670	7.08	1.69	2.07	76.97	1.14	11.55	1.85	6	35.91	14.88	
Mediterranean Spring	25	3513	do	4.640	7.53	1.67	2.61	72.80	1.65	13.30	2.21	6	34.73	10.49	
China Tea	26	3514	do	5.000	7.38	1.18	2.58	73.27	1.60	13.30	2.13	6	10.44	10.24	
Chili	27	3515	Yellow	4.440	6.35	1.61	2.02	77.16	1.25	11.38	1.82	6	35.35	13.34	
China Spring	28	3516	Dark amber	3.900	6.39	1.53	2.49	74.24	1.65	14.00	2.24	6	31.96	11.60	
Egyptian Fife	29	3517	Yellow and amber	3.840	6.98	1.61	2.11	75.64	1.23	12.43	1.99	6	27.81	10.82	
Saxon Fife	29	3518	Red	3.690	6.51	1.18	2.38	73.98	1.50	14.35	2.30	6	30.59	14.63	
Dominion	30	3519	Red and yellow	4.110	6.26	1.73	2.22	74.84	1.63	13.30	2.13	6	41.29	14.02	
Prussian	31	3520	Dark amber	4.300	7.01	1.75	1.22	76.61	2.10	10.15	1.62	6	29.02	9.35	
Pringle	34	3521	Light amber	4.300	6.97	1.91	1.95	75.09	1.63	11.90	1.90	6	25.42	8.44	
White Chaff Hedgerow	41	3522	Yellow and amber	3.170	5.95	1.85	2.43	78.85	1.20	9.98	1.60	6	33.02	11.81	
Italian	43	3523	Red and yellow	3.020	6.92	1.91	2.17	75.50	1.95	11.90	1.90	6	24.22	8.19	
Hybrid No. 10	51	3524	Pale yellow	4.690	8.57	1.75	1.78	78.60	1.85	9.45	1.51	5			
Nox No. 1	54	3525	Yellow and amber	3.980	6.35	1.62	2.08	77.07	1.33	11.55	1.85	5	27.98	9.83	
Hybrid No. 13	56	3526	Amber and amber	3.169	7.13	1.78	2.50	74.07	1.48	12.95	2.07	5	34.18	12.44	
Hybrid No. 15	57	3527	Yellow and amber	3.200	8.19	1.75	2.32	74.23	1.43	11.38	1.82	5			
Hybrid No. 16	58	3528	Red and amber	4.110	7.04	1.95	2.27	75.18	1.58	12.25	1.96	5	41.60	13.12	
Hybrid No. 17	59	3529	Red	4.740	7.00	1.60	2.55	75.45	1.15	14.18	2.27	5	39.68	14.04	
Androla Amber	66	3530	Red and amber	3.790	8.07	1.90	2.61	71.64	1.60	12.76	2.04	3	36.30	12.83	
Red Clawson	113	3531	Dark amber	3.660	7.51	1.85	2.19	74.06	1.61	11.63	1.79	3	38.00	13.24	
Big Mary	117	3532	Dark yellow	4.710	7.16	2.05	2.09	75.87	1.03	12.08	1.93	3	28.45	9.96	
Hybrid No. 26	122	3533	Light amber	5.339	8.12	1.95	2.01	74.39	1.45	12.08	1.93	3	36.60	12.01	
Hybrid No. 28	124	3534	Dark yellow	4.683	9.15	2.10	2.82	73.43	1.80	11.20	1.79	3	33.01	11.63	
Hybrid No. 33	129	3535	do	3.586	8.79	1.84	2.31	76.30	1.75	9.80	1.57	3	26.06	9.24	
Hybrid No. 34	130	3536	Amber, glassy, and shriveled	5.020	8.42	2.25	2.53	73. 9	1.68	12.08	1.93	3	33.49	11.70	
Casaca	121	3537	Red	4.299	8.65	2.10	1.99	73.31	1.05	11.73	1.88	3	38.64	12.94	
Monmouth	148	3538	Light red	3.430	8.24	2.05	2.68	72.70	1.55	12.74	2.04	2	35.32	12.82	
Russian Spring	149	3539	Red	3.880	8.41	1.95	2.36	72.01	1.79	13.48	2.16	3	35.26	13.00	
Vermillion	150	3540	do	3.500	7.84	2.00	2.34	71.49	1.63	14.70	2.35	8	35.90	12.89	Good.

152	3541	Edenton Fife	...do	4.0100	9.33	1.93	2.50	71.30	1.84	13.30	2.13	37.09	3	12.92	Poor.
153	3542	Nox 2	Yellow and amber	4.1700	7.52	2.30	2.16	75.34	1.30	11.38	1.82	36.50	3	12.82	Good.
156	3543	Nox 4	Light red	4.6700	8.13	1.65	2.51	74.51	1.30	11.00	1.90	29.90	3	10.29	Very bad.
156	3544	Nox 3	Amber, glassy, and shriveled	5.5035	8.43	2.05	2.80	70.79	1.40	14.53	2.32	37.86	3	14.40	Good.
157	3545	Nox 5	Amber and yellow	4.2390	8.48	1.45	2.21	74.31	1.30	12.25	1.96	32.62	3	11.32	Medium.
158	3546	Pringle No. 17	Yellow and amber	4.1670	7.94	2.00	2.73	73.03	1.70	12.60	2.02	34.25	3	12.28	Do.
160	3547	Wales	Light amber	5.0735	7.74	1.50	1.97	70.19	1.55	10.85	1.74	29.64	3	9.59	Poor.
163	3548	Northcotes Improved	Yellow	3.5760	7.66	1.95	1.34	75.62	1.93	10.50	1.68	12.30	3	4.21	Very bad.
164	3549	Northcotes Amber	Light red	4.1200	7.46	1.60	2.38	76.01	1.25	10.85	1.74	29.04	3	9.64	Good.
108	3550	Black Chaff	Red	4.2200	7.53	1.50	2.03	75.54	1.35	11.20	1.79	30.77	3	10.87	Puffy.
169	3551	Hybrid No. 35	Amber and yellow	3.8000	8.28	1.50	2.43	76.57	1.48	10.50	1.68	20.59	2	10.18	Medium.
171	3552	Hebron	...do	3.5000	7.69	2.10	1.90	72.96	1.35	14.00	2.24	33.01	2	12.23	Do.
173	3553	Mediterranean White	Deep yellow	2.5800	7.74	1.75	1.95	73.93	1.50	13.13	2.10	33.60	2	11.83	
175	3554	French Imperial	Red	4.8800	7.00	2.00	2.74	73.99	1.65	12.00	2.02	17.15	2	7.05	Very bad.
176	3555	Nebraska	Amber	4.4400	7.08	2.15	2.10	72.86	1.98	13.83	2.21	37.46	2	12.49	Medium good.
177	3556	White North Carolina	Light red	4.4000	6.90	1.50	2.52	74.20	1.75	13.13	2.10	31.14	2	11.12	Do.
178	3557	Kirel	Deep yellow	4.2200	7.18	1.95	2.35	72.57	1.95	14.00	2.24	34.58	2	12.19	Do.
180	3558	Baltimore	Light red	5.0600	7.00	2.05	2.29	73.45	1.55	14.00	2.02	31.83	2	11.68	Medium.
181	3559	Davis	...do	4.2200	7.12	1.25	1.06	72.71	1.38	14.88	2.38	43.16	2	13.08	Good.
183	3560	Gold Premium	...do	4.1290	6.80	1.95	2.56	72.94	1.75	14.00	2.24	36.08	2	12.46	Do.
184	3561	Hicks Prolific	Red	3.8900	6.98	1.45	2.10	75.04	1.48	12.78	2.02	33.29	2	11.48	Do.
186	3562	Winter green	Amber	3.9300	7.11	1.35	1.95	74.81	1.75	13.30	2.13	39.07	2	13.43	Do.
192	3563	Geiger	...do	2.2400	6.23	1.60	2.25	75.26	1.38	13.13	2.10	35.57	2	12.57	Medium good.
193	3564	Hybrid No. 37	Amber and yellow	3.8500	6.08	2.05	2.58	74.81	1.58	12.43	1.99	31.96	2	11.56	Very bad.
194	3565	Sea Island	Red	4.2200	6.77	1.40	2.07	75.75	1.78	12.25	1.96	31.05	2	11.18	Medium.
195	3566	Edenton	Amber	5.1800	7.69	1.65	2.56	74.25	1.54	12.60	2.02	33.49	2	11.58	Do.
196	3567	Winnipeg Russian	Light red	4.1200	9.17	1.83	1.93	71.25	1.85	12.08	1.93	33.49	2	11.62	Shriveled.
198	3568	Manitoba	Red	5.5600	8.09	2.05	2.25	72.23	1.80	12.50	1.98	34.40	2	14.29	Poor.
197	3569	Winnipeg	Deep amber, yellow, glassy	5.5600	7.39	2.05	2.84	72.67	1.78	14.18	2.27	32.46	2	13.03	Do.
200	3570	Hallet's Pedigree	Amber and yellow	3.8800	8.31	2.00	2.63	71.81	1.95	14.08	2.27	22.90	2	0.31	Bad.
213	3571	China No. 2	Amber	1.8000	8.04	2.35	3.20	69.71	1.75	15.05	2.41	41.82	2	14.60	Good.
214	3572	Mo. Turkey		4.0000						15.25	1.96		1		
215	3573	Mo. Mediterranean	Light red	4.4800	8.68	2.15	2.21	71.21	1.75	14.00	2.24	36.98	1	13.87	Very good.
222	3574	Scotish Fife	Red	3.4400	8.13	1.90	2.50	71.67	1.80	14.00	2.24	46.25	1	16.97	Do.
223	3575	Rye	Dark and light red	4.7600	7.96	1.95	2.04	73.03	1.72	13.30	2.13		1		
233	3576	Sandomirka	Dark red	4.0600	7.54	1.90	2.36	73.23	1.90	12.95	2.07		1		
235	3577	Hopetown	Amber	4.5000	6.97	.95	2.17	72.53	2.08	13.30	2.13		1		

13734—No 9——2

The data in the preceding tables have been averaged for comparison with the averages of previous years as well as of those wheats which had been grown different lengths of time in Colorado.

Average composition of Colorado wheat grown in 1884.

	Number.	Weight per bushel.	Weight per 100 grains.	Water.	Ash.	Oil.	Carbohydrates.	Fiber.	Albuminoids.	Nitrogen.	Gluten. Moist.	Gluten. Dry.
		Lbs.	*Grams.*	*P. ct.*	*P. ct.*	*P. ct.*	*P. ct.*	*P. ct.*	*P. ct.*	*P. ct.*	*P. ct.*	*P. ct.*
All varieties....	77	65.2	4.222	7.54	1.81	2.29	74.19	1.64	12.53	2.00	33.31	10.42
Sixth season....	24	65.2	4.408	7.15	1.70	2.24	74.83	1.64	12.44	1.99	32.96	10.31
Fifth season....	7	64.4	4.167	7.19	1.75	2.32	75.27	1.49	11.98	1.92	35.75	12.45
Third season ...	19	64.7	4.402	8.11	2.01	2.34	73.90	1.59	12.05	1.93	34.33	12.05
Second season ..	21	65.6	3.968	7.34	1.81	2.32	73.96	1.67	12.90	2.06	32.50	11.65
First season	7	66.5	4.203	8.37	1.88	2.25	71.90	1.83	13.77	2.20	42.68	15.15

The average for the seventy-seven varieties grown in 1884 when compared with that of other years shows that in size and percentage of albuminoids, although there has been an advance over 1883, the wheats of that year are not equal to those of 1881 and 1882.

Average composition of Colorado wheats.

	1881.	1882.	1883.	1884.
Weight of 100 grains..........................grams..	4.865	4.283	3.941	4.222
Water...per cent..	9.86	8.80	9.38	7.54
Ash...do ...	2.28	1.99	2.09	1.81
Oil..do ...	2.41	2.38	.....	2.29
Carbhydrates.......................................do ...	70.48	72.03	76.79	74.19
Crude fiber..do ...	1.57	1.76	....	1.64
Albuminoids..do ...	13.40	13.04	11.74	12.53
Total..	100.00	100.00	100.00	100.00
Nitrogen...do ...	2.14	2.09	1.88	2.00
Moist gluten.......................................do ...	33.12	34.69	....	33.31
Dry gluten..do ...	11.74	12.89	....	10.42

It would perhaps be unsafe to draw any definite conclusions from these averages, but they would seem to show that peculiarities of season are most influential on the composition of the grain.

Examined in connection with the individual analyses and with regard to the characteristics of the several seasons of growth it would appear that the low percentage of albuminoids in 1884 may be due to the fact that having fallen to 11.74 in 1883, the wheats were unable to recover more than to 12.53 in 1884. If this is the case the effects of this bad season and set back in 1883 may be overcome in 1885. Analysis of that year's crop will decide this.

Then, the inquiry may be made as to what influence on this average is due to the continued growth of the grain on one soil for a number of years. To examine this question the averages by seasons of growth were calculated. From these one learns that the wheats of the first two seasons growth are richer in albuminoids than those which have been raised a longer time in Colorado. In the case of the wheats grown for the first time in the State the higher figures are probably due to the fact that the seed had not been injured by the hailstorm which had affected the others, and they therefore produced a grain as rich as that from seed introduced in 1881 and 1882. Why, however, there should be a decrease from the second to the fifth season and increase in the sixth is not so easy to say. The difference is small and may be due to peculiarities in the varieties rather than other conditions.

To discover what the deterioration may have been for particular varieties the analyses of all wheats which have been made more than once are tabulated together on the following page:

Name.	Collection number.	Serial number.	Color.	Weight of 100 grains.	Water.	Ash.	Albuminoids.	Nitrogen.	Seasons.	Number of seasons.
				Grms.	P. ct.	P.c.	P. ct.	P.c.		
Oregon Club	10	738	Yellow	4.434	9.59	1.91	12.25	1.96	1881	3
Do	10	2127	...do	3.714	8.75	2.10	11.38	1.82	1883	5
Do	10	3500	Light amber	3.647	6.93	1.98	11.20	1.79	1884	6
Australian Hard	11	731	Yellow	5.506	9.78	1.85	11.19	1.79	1881	3
Do	11	3501	Light amber	4.041	7.46	2.05	11.73	1.88	1884	6
Sonora	12	739	Yellow	4.739	10.17	2.02	14.18	2.27	1881	3
Do	12	2133	...do	3.618	9.12	1.96	12.78	2.04	1883	5
Do	12	3502	...do	3.830	7.31	1.90	12.25	1.96	1884	6
White Mexican	13	729	...do		9.91	2.60	13.81	2.21	1881	3
Do	13	2128	...do	4.442	8.35	2.20	11.90	1.90	1883	5
Do	13	3503	...do	4.890	7.27	2.05	11.55	1.85	1884	6
Improved Fife	14	2129	Amber	3.784	9.28	2.04	13.83	2.21	1883	5
Do	14	3504	Light amber	3.672	8.72	1.78	14.18	2.27	1884	6
Rio Grande	17	735	Red	5.906	9.51	2.08	14.69	2.35	1881	3
Do	17	2134	do	4.162	8.89	2.03	12.95	2.07	1883	5
Do	17	3506	Amber	4.743	8.74	1.52	12.43	1.99	1884	6
Judkin	19	730	Red		9.75	2.57	12.25	1.96	1881	3
Do	19	2137	Amber	3.761	9.13	1.91	11.55	1.85	1883	5
Do	19	3508	Dark amber	3.920	7.63	1.94	12.25	1.96	1884	6
Lost Nation	20	741	Red	3.851	10.24	2.17	12.93	2.07	1881	3
Do	20	2139	Amber	3.739	9.93	1.87	11.55	1.85	1883	5
Do	20	3509	...do	4.147	7.29	1.53	12.08	1.93	1884	6
Touzelle	21	736	Yellow	5.214	10.23	2.10	13.50	2.16	1881	3
Do	21	2141	.do	4.247	10.73	2.12	13.30	2.13	1883	5
Do	21	3510	Light amber	4.300	6.98	1.79	14.18	2.27	1884	6
Australian Club	22	2142	Yellow	4.425	8.97	1.97	11.03	1.76	1883	5
Do	22	3511	Mixed amber and white	4.536	7.16	1.16	11.55	1.85	1884	6
Pringles No. 6	33	742	Yellow	5.145	9.89	2.12	13.13	2.10	1881	3
Do	33	2153	...do	4.651	9.30	2.08	13.65	2.18	1883	5
Pringles No. 7	34	743	Amber	4.636	9.89	2.23	15.25	2.44	1881	3
Do	34	2154	Yellow	3.968	9.15	2.05	12.08	1.93	1883	5
Centennial	40	727			9.66	2.35	12.06	1.93	1881	3
Do	40	2150	Yellow	5.878	8.60	2.10	11.55	1.85	1883	5
White Chaff, Hedge Row	41	745	...do	4.072	9.07	2.08	13.62	2.18	1881	3
Do	41	2160	do	2.838	9.16	2.02	11.73	1.88	1883	5
Do	41	3522	Yellow and amber	3.170	5.95	1.50	9.98	1.60	1884	6
Hybrid No. 10	51	719	Amber		9.72	2.28	13.75	2.20	1881	3
Do	51	2126	Yellow	5.024	8.68	2.26	11.03	1.76	1883	3
Do	51	3524	Pale yellow	4.690	9.57	1.75	9.45	1.51	1884	6
Hybrid No. 13	56	2189	Red	3.699	10.27	2.10	10.68	1.71	1883	4
Do	56	3526	Amber	3.660	7.13	1.28	12.95	2.07	1884	5
Hybrid No. 15	57	720	Red		10.07	1.93	12.25	1.96	1881	2
Do	57	2131	... do	3.572	8.87	2.03	11.73	1.88	1883	4
Do	57	3527	Yellow and amber	3.200	8.19	1.75	12.08	1.93	1884	5

Name.	Collection number.	Serial number.	Color.	Weight of 100 grains.	Water.	Ash.	Albuminoids.	Nitrogen.	Seasons.	Number of seasons.
				Grms.	P. ct.	P. c.	P. ct.	P. c.		
Hybrid No. 16	58	721	Red	4.824	9.53	2.04	11.75	1.8s	1881	2
Do	58	2132	Amber	5.086	8.70	2.13	11.03	1.76	1883	4
Do	58	3528	Red and amber	4.110	7.04	1.95	11.38	1.82	1884	5
Hybrid No. 17	59	722	Amber	5.137	9.93	2.07	13.62	2.18	1881	2
Do	59	2135	Red	4.818	8.90	2.23	14.35	2.30	1883	4
Do	59	3529	...do	4.740	7.00	1.60	12.25	1.96	1884	5
Hedge Row, Red Chaff	69	746	Amber	4.499	9.17	2.59	12.94	2.07	1881	3
Do	09	2161	Yellow	4.008	9.18	2.19	12.95	2.07	1883	5
Fountain	71	732	...do	5.100	10.58	2.70	13.62	2.18	1881	3
Do	71	2162	...do	4.191	8.27	2.14	11.90	1.90	1883	5
White Chaff	74	747	Red	4.214	9.57	2.03	14.04	2.25	1881	3
Do	74	2163	. do	3.252	7.95	2.05	12.08	1.93	1883	5
Perfection	76	733	Yellow	5.536	9.93	1.99	14.18	2.27	1881	2
Do	76	2164	...do	5.032	10.29	2.08	12.95	2.07	1883	4
German Fife	77	737	Red	5.368	10.42	2.31	15.06	2.41	1881	2
Do	77	2168	Amber	4.546	10.05	2.28	12.60	2.02	1883	4
Triticum	79	748	Yellow	5.754	10.02	2.07	13.62	2.18	1881	2
Do	79	2165	...do	4.861	8.98	2.02	14.00	2.24	1883	4
Russian Durum	81	749	Amber	5.024	9.91	2.32	15.25	2.44	1881	2
Do	81	2166	Yellow	4.761	8.70	2.10	14.35	2.30	1883	4
Meekin's	88	751	Red	5.193	9.38	2.53	15.15	2.43	1881	2
Do	88	2167	...do	4.414	10.15	2.05	13.48	2.16	1883	4
Hybrid No. 26	122	2146	Yellow	3.987	9.40	2.20	14.3g	2.38	1883	2
Do	122	3533	Light amber	5.339	8.12	1.93	12.08	1.93	1884	3
Hybrid No. 28	124	2148	Yellow	3.827	9.32	2.28	9.98	1.60	1883	2
Do	124	3534	Dark yellow	4.683	9.15	2.10	11.20	1.79	1884	3
Hybrid No. 33	129	2152	Yellow	2.716	10.15	1.87	8.93	1.43	1883	2
Do	129	3535	Dark yellow	3.587	8.00	1.84	9.80	1.57	1884	3
Hybrid No. 34	130	2155	Amber	5.179	8.82	2.43	12.60	2.02	1883	2
Do	130	3536	Amber and glassy	6.620	8.42	2.25	12.08	1.93	1884	3
Russian, Spring	149	2171	Amber	3.438	8.92	2.31	12.78	2.04	1882	1
Do	149	2172	...do	3.985	9.68	2.14	12.25	1.96	1883	2
Do	149	3539	Red	3.880	8.41	1.95	13.48	2.16	1884	3
Hybrid No. 35	169	2156	Yellow	3.055	9.37	2.27	10.50	1.68	1883	1
Do	169	3551	Amber and yellow	3.800	7.53	1.50	10.50	1.68	1884	2
Mediterranean White	173	2174	Yellow	4.182	9.69	2.17	11.20	1.79	1883	1
Do	173	3553	White	5.580	7.74	1.75	13.13	2.10	1884	2
French Imperial	175	2178	Amber	4.594	9.55	1.95	12.95	2.07	1883	1
Do	175	3554	Red	4.880	7.00	2.00	12.60	2.02	1884	2
Gold Premium	183	2184	Yellow	3.818	9.44	2.17	11.38	1.82	1883	1
Do	183	3560	Light red	4.120	6.80	1.95	14.00	2.24	1884	2
Hick's Prolific	184	2186	Amber	2.879	9.21	2.04	10.33	1.65	1883	1
Do	184	3561	Red	3.890	6.88	1.45	12.78	2.02	1884	2
Geiger	192	2188	Yellow	4.064	9.92	2.20	14.33	2.32	1883	1
Do	192	3563	Amber	4.240	6.23	2.00	13.13	2.10	1884	2
Hybrid No. 37	193	2158	Yellow	3.559	10.72	2.44	11.90	1.90	1883	1
Do	193	3564	Amber and yellow	3.850	6.08	2.05	12.20	1.96	1884	2

Among the varieties which were analyzed in 1884, and also previously, six have shown a tendency to continued degeneration in their percentages of nitrogen and size. The rest have shown signs of improvement or remained stationary. The changes, then, which have been observed from year to year must be attributed to season and not to the soil, although continued cropping on one soil, even with fertilizers, appears from the experiments of Lawes and Gilbert to somewhat diminish the percentage of nitrogen. Another year's crop will furnish interesting data upon this subject, no doubt confirming the views of the experimenters just mentioned that season has a greater effect upon grain than any other condition.

Among these analyses are found samples of wheat which have the greatest weight per bushel and per hundred grains of any which have been examined. These extremes are not, however, coincident, as may be seen from the following figures:

Extremes among Colorado wheats of 1884.

	Highest.	Number.	Lowest.	Number.
Yield per acre .... bushels..	86¾	3560	21½	3575
Weight per bushel .... pounds..	68.6	3576	62.2	3534
Weight per 100 grains .... grams..	6.200	3569	3.160	3526
Albuminoids .... per cent..	14.88	3559	9.45	3524

The weight per bushel is dependent on various causes. High weight is almost, if not always, an evidence of high quality, but not always of a large, plump, well-matured grain. The hard red spring wheat of the Northwest, which is small in size, and not well matured in the sense of having a plump berry, with its usual amount of starch, is very heavy in its weight per bushel, while the large full wheat of Oregon, which is very starchy, is light in weight.

The following data show the variation:

Weight per bushel, &c., of hard, soft, and immature wheats.

HARD RED SPRING WHEAT.

No.	State.	Weight per bushel.	Weight per 100 grains.	Yield.	Quality.	Albuminoids.
		Pounds.	Grams.	Bush.		Per cent.
1863	Dakota	65.3	3.312	25½	Good	14.53
1864	......do	66.5	2.802	26½	No. 1	15.23
1865	......do	66.2	3.368	27	......do	17.33
1866	......do	65.2	3.389	27¼	......do	14.00
1867	......do	65.2	2.921	36	......do	14.35
1868	Minnesota	65.5	2.780	(?)	......do	16.35
1869	Dakota	66.8	3.700	(?)	......do	16.28
2109	Manitoba	67.1	3.465	(?)	......do	13.48
2111	Dakota	63.4	3.074	(?)	......do	18.03
1644	Minnesota	64.9	3.331	(?)	Frozen	13.65
2107	......do	64.3	2.926	(?)	No. 1	13.83

SOFT WHITE OREGON WHEATS.

772	Oregon	57.2	4.253	......	Extra	8.58
773	......do	59.8	5.144	......	......do	8.05

IMPORTED SOFT WHEAT.

Weight per bushel, &c., of hard, soft, and immature wheat—Continued.

OTHER SOFT WHEATS.

No.	State.	Weight per bushel.	Weight per 100 grains.	Yield.	Quality.	Albuminoids.
		Pounds.	*Grams.*	*Bush.*		*Per cent.*
832	Pennsylvania	60.4	2.710	44	Ordinary	9.98
759	Missouri	62.7	3.860		do	11.19
1288	Pennsylvania	62.1	2.526		do	10.50
1293	Michigan	62.1	4.196		do	10.85
1355	Maryland	63.4	3.077		do	10.85
1356	North Carolina	66.2	3.653		do	10.55
1853	West Virginia	64.5	3.392	15	Good	11.30
2112	Virginia	65.0	3.569	20	do	12.60

IMMATURE AND POOR WHEATS.

No.	State.	Weight per bushel.	Weight per 100 grains.	Yield.	Quality.	Albuminoids.
1804	Alabama	52.3	2.011	3.5	Poor	10.85
1305	do	62.3	3.710	10.3	Fair	10.85
1806	do	49.8	2.242	5.2	Bad	9.98
1809	do	63.5	3.486	5.3	Fair	11.03
1812	do	48.1	2.166	2.8	Bad	9.80
1813	do	57.0	2.675	1.6	Poor	11.38

AVERAGE OF 42 POOR WHEATS FROM OHIO IN 1883.

No.	State.	Weight per bushel.	Weight per 100 grains.	Yield.	Quality.	Albuminoids.
2701–2742		56.6	3.458	39.3	Shriveled	12.89

WHEATS WITH HIGHEST AND LOWEST ALBUMEN AND LARGEST SIZE.

No.	State.	Weight per bushel.	Weight per 100 grains.	Yield.	Quality.	Albuminoids.
2111	Dakota	63.4	3.074		High albumen	18.03
1854	Washington Territory	63.5	2.584		Low albumen	7.70
3536	Colorado	64.4	5.560			12.08

HIGHEST WEIGHT PER BUSHEL.

No.	State.	Weight per bushel.	Weight per 100 grains.	Yield.	Quality.	Albuminoids.
3570	Colorado	68.6	4.000		Hard red	12.95

LOWEST WEIGHT PER BUSHEL.

No.	State.	Weight per bushel.	Weight per 100 grains.	Yield.	Quality.	Albuminoids.
1812	Alabama	48	2.166		Immature	9.80

From these figures, which have been obtained by weighing miniature bushels which were graduated by comparison with the weight of large amounts of grain in struck bushels, it appears that hard spring wheat will average about 65½ pounds per bushel, soft white Oregon 58½ pounds, the ordinary soft wheat of the East 62.5, the poorly-matured grain of Alabama 55.5, the crop of 1883 in Ohio 56.6, while we have seen that the large plump Colorado grain weighs 65.2 pounds. The averages for different seasons in Colorado vary directly as the percentages of albuminoids, although among the less fully matured grain the lighter often contains more nitrogen from lack of starch, as in the case of the Ohio crop of 1883. This was found to be the case by Lawes and Gilbert in their experiments, but does not always hold true, as may be seen among the Alabama wheats and some others. The Oregon wheats finely matured, rich in starch, and low in nitrogen, which are very spongy and light in weight, are illustrative of this point.

Conditions of growth and seed formation are so many and so varied that what may be true for one locality will often not apply to another which is far distant.

RELIABILITY OF SPECIMENS AND SAMPLING.

The question has been raised as to whether any specimen or sample of wheat would represent the average composition of a field or large crop, or of a large mass of wheat in elevator, for instance, and whether the analyses of the specimens which have been examined in this and previous reports could be relied on on this account.

An attempt has been made to solve this question, and with satisfactory results. In Bulletin No. 1 of this division analyses are given of two samples of wheat from the same lot of grain purchased by the Department as seed, the one selected in 1881 and the other in 1882, and analyzed without it being known to any one that they were intended to be identical. The results were closer than would probably be the case in most sampling.

Red Mediterranean wheat.

	1882.	1883.
	Per cent.	Per cent.
Water	9.83	9.88
Ash	1.70	1.62
Oil	2.21	2.06
Carbhydrates	73.73	73.80
Crude fiber	1.68	1.79
Albuminoids	10.85	10.85

To decide as to variations in composition in different parts of the same field and of the same farm, and of different varieties on the same farm and of differently developed heads and sized kernels of the same variety, personal selections were made from a wheat farm in Carroll County, Maryland, belonging to Mr. Alastair P. Gordon-Cumming.

The specimens may be described as follows, with a determination of albuminoids—a point which, it was believed, will settle any large variation in composition:

From a field of Fultz, bottom land, best quality.

Serial number.	Number of heads.	Length of head in inches.	Average weight in grams.	Number of grains of wheat.	Weight of grain in grams.	Per cent. of grain.	Weight per 100.	Per cent. of albumen.	Name.
2769	21		0.80	325	14.67	79.3	4.517	9.80	Rakings.

From twenty-two average heads were selected:

2770[1]	1	4.0	.89	30	.535		1.621	12.78	Longest, not well filled.
2770[2]	1	3.8	1.89	45	1.282		2.085	11.81	Next longest, well filled.
2770[3]	8	3.5	1.46	285	9.055		3.177	12.78	Long.
2770[4]	9	3.3	1.21	273	8.035		2.943	12.78	Short.
2770[5]	3	3.0	1.04	73	2.260		3.096	12.60	Shortest.

A patch of white Mediterranean seed from Department, second year's growth.

Serial No. 2768, 33 heads, weighing 37.5 grams and yielding 567 grains, or 75.2 per cent., weighing 28.197 grams, of which 461 were sound and 106 sprouted in the stack.

The sound weighed per 100, 4.875 grams; the sprouted, 5.400, and contained albuminoids; the sound, 12.08 per cent.; the sprouted, 13.48.

A field of Fultz, from a different portion of the same farm, gave among 14 average heads, weighing 391 grains:

Serial number.		Number of grains.	Weight.	Weight per 100.	Albuminoids.
2771[1]	Large plump grains	240	8.792	3.663	14.00
2771[2]	Smaller grains	150	4.085	2.723	11.88

Among the Fultz sports were found:

2772[1]	Bearded brown chaff			4.184	11.03
2772[2]	Smooth brown chaff			3.095	14.00

The results show that where the divisions have been made on marked characteristics there is a difference in composition; but that for averages from the same field, even where some physical differences could be noted, there is little variation on analysis. Three of six samples from a field of Fultz were exactly alike in their percentage of albuminoids, another was only .18 per cent. different, or practically the same, while the rakings from the field were, as might be expected, low in albuminoids. One selected head also fell below the average composition for some unexplained reason. In this field of Fultz, therefore, there seems to be sufficient evidence to give us confidence in our results.

The next samples were taken from a shock of wheat, and the grain was found on preparation for analysis to have sprouted. It was therefore divided into two parts. The grain which sprouted was the heavier and best developed and contained the most albuminoids. This is also the case in another field of Fultz on the same farm, where an average sample was divided into large and small grains, the larger having the most albuminoids. That this is not by any means always the case, however, it seems fair to believe from our experience with high relative proportion of nitrogen in specimens of shriveled wheat from other parts of the country. These kernels were none of them shrivelled; on the contrary, plump, and that some were merely more vigorous than others must stand as an explanation.

Sports or stragglers in the same field of Fultz were found to vary very largely from each other and a little more than the different-sized grains of Fultz. This must be attributed to peculiarities in the variety and their different ability to assimilate nitrogen under the circumstances.

These remarks must be regarded as suggestious only, as any absolute interpretation of the results is impossible. They serve, however, to show the constancy of the average composition of an average head, and of the average of the crop.

CHARACTERISTICS OF THE WHEAT GRAIN.

From observations in this and previous reports it may be said that of all grain wheat is probably the most susceptible to its environment. Oats in certain directions are more variable, but in their general characteristics are much more permanent, as will appear in subsequent pages. The inherent tendency to change which is found in all grains is most prominent in wheat. It may be fostered by selection and by modifying such of the conditions of environment as it is in the power of man to affect.

The most powerful element to contend with is the character of the season or unfavorable climatic conditions. The injury done in this way is well illustrated in Colorado, and it would seem advisable in such cases to seek seed from a source where everything had been favorable, and begin selection again.

It must be borne in mind that selection must be kept up continuously, and that reversion takes place more easily than improvement. It took but one season to seriously injure Professor Blount's wheats, but it will be two or more years before they have recovered from that injury. Hallett in England was able to make his celebrated pedigree wheat by selection, carried on through many years, but the same wheat grown by the ordinary farmer under unfavorable conditions for a few years without care has reverted to an ordinary sort of grain.

The effect of climate is well illustrated by four specimens of wheat which are to be seen in the collection of the chemical division. Two of these were from Oregon and Dakota some years ago, and present the most extreme contrast which can be found in this variable grain. One is light yellow, plump, and starchy, and shows on analysis a very small proportion of albuminoids; the other is one of the small, hard, and dark-colored spring wheats of Dakota, which are rich in albuminoids. Between these stand two specimens from Colorado, which have been raised from seed similar to the Oregon and Dakota wheat. They are scarcely distinguishable except by a slight difference in color. The Colorado climate is such as to have modified these two seed wheats, until after a few years' growth they are hardly distinguishable in the kernel.

All localities having widely different climates, soils, or other conditions produce their peculiar varieties and modify those which are brought to them.

The result of these tendencies to change and reversion from lack of care in seed selection or other case has led to the practice of change of seed among farmers. A source is sought where either through greater care or more favorable conditions the variety desired has been able to hold its own. Sometimes this change is rendered necessary by conditions which are beyond the power of man to modify. As an example, No. 10 of Professor Blount's wheats, known as "Oregon Club," a white variety from Oregon, has been deteriorating every year since it has been grown in Colorado, whereas if the seed had been supplied every season directly from Oregon the quality would probably have remained the same. In extension of this illustration, the fact may be mentioned that annual renewal of the seed from a desirable and favorable source often makes it possible to raise cereals where otherwise the climatic conditions would render their cultivation impossible through rapid reversion. This is particularly the case with extremes in latitude, the effect of which is found not so much upon the composition of the crop as on the yield and size of the grain. In the South the warmer climate, together, of course, with poorer soil and cultivation in many instances, reduces the yield. The average in different States is given by Mr. Dodge as follows:

Yield per acre of wheat.

State.	Per cent.	State.	Per cent.	State.	Per cent.
Maine	15.2	South Carolina	5.6	Michigan	19.5
New Hampshire	15.0	Georgia	6.6	Indiana	18.0
Vermont	16.3	Florida	5.2	Illinois	15.9
Massachusetts	16.4	Alabama	5.7	Wisconsin	12.8
Rhode Island	14.1	Mississippi	5.0	Minnesota	11.4
Connecticut	17.6	Nevada	16.8	Iowa	10.2
New York	15.7	Louisiana	9.4	Missouri	12.0
New Jersey	12.7	Texas	6.8	Kansas	9.3
Pennsylvania	13.5	Arkansas	6.2	Nebraska	9.4
Delaware	13.4	Tennessee	6.1	California	22.0
Maryland	14.1	West Virginia	10.2	Oregon	15.8
Virginia	8.7	Kentucky	9.8	Colorado	18.9
North Carolina	5.2	Ohio	18.0		

It must be remembered, however, that three quarters of the wheat crop has been produced in the ten States of Illinois, Indiana, Ohio, Michigan, Minnesota, Iowa, California, Missouri, Wisconsin, and Pennsylvania, and that a State like Minnesota must not be considered as furnishing the largest part of the supply merely because wheat is the prevailing crop in that State.

Having shown the conditions under which unfavorable and favorable variations occur, it is hoped that these investigations will be the means of aiding those who are engaged in the improvement of the yield and quality of the crop of our country.

It seems proper in this place to allude also to the immense amount of the best food elements of our soils which are yearly being taken from the farm and exported from our ports in the shape of nitrogen and the mineral constituents of the grain, the loss of which is continually rendering our wheat lands poorer and forcing the cultivation into new parts of the country where the soil is still of virgin richness. If grain is sold off the farm the loss of nitrogen and minerals must be replaced by fertilizers. In the East this is already done, but in the West it seems that nothing but experience of wasting fertility will teach the lesson.

OATS.

Oats, the third in importance of our cereal crops, as far as production is concerned, are grown under as varied conditions as any of them and are as a crop the most variable in their appearance. They will grow and can be made to pay on almost any soil, and, although flourishing in cold climates, can be successfully raised in the far South by sowing as a winter grain and so reaching maturity in the cool part of the year.

In consequence of these variations in the conditions of growth there are to be found the greatest differences in weight and size of the grain, its plumpness, and the relative proportion of kernel and husk. Dependent on these differences many classifications have been proposed, but as there seems to be a regular gradation from the one extreme of the white potato oats to the other of red rust proof, there seems to be no definite basis for varieties due to color, shape of the grain, or plumpness. Botanically, there seem to be three varieties recognized—the common *Avena sativa* L., and two others, *A. orientals* Schb., having the kernels all on one side of the stem, and *A. nuda* L., to the grain of which the husks or chaff are not adherent.

For our consideration, from a chemical and physical point of view, these distinctions are of small importance, as the same variations are found among each species.

To the farmer the most important characteristic, and the one by which this grain is usually valued, is its weight per bushel. In close relation to this is the proportion of kernel to husk—a point which has been little, if at all, investigated. In the specimens which have been collected from the most prominent regions where oats are grown these characteristics have been determined, as well as the size and weight of the kernels, with the purpose of studying not only the way in which they are affected by surrounding causes, but also their relation to the composition of the grain.

The sources of the specimens examined, their color and shape, and other physical characteristics are here presented.

Sources of specimens of oats.

State	Serial No.	Name	Sown	Harvested	County	Post-office	Sender	Remarks
Alabama	3001	Red Rust Proof	Sept. 15 to Nov. 15	June	Lawrence	Wheeler	J. J. Barclay	
	3002	...do	Aug. to Feb	June	Talladega	Talladega	H. M. Burt	
	3003	...do	Oct. to Jan	May to June	Barbour	Hawkinsville	H. Hawkins	
	3007	Brewington Rust Proof	November	June 10	Lee	Salem	G. L. Webster	
	3008	Imp. Red Rust Proof	Sept. to Dec					
California	3012	Red Rust Proof	Jan. to Mar	May 20	Dallas	Selma	Joseph Hardie	
	3016	White Oats	Fall or Spring	May to June	Hempstead	Washington	A. H. Carrigan	"Feeding" from warehouse.
			Feb. to Mar	End of July	Contra Costa	Martinez	J. Strentzel	
Colorado	3020	Welcome	May 10	Aug. 14	Douglas	Castle Rock	L. W. Wells	
Connecticut	3021	Russian White (fr. Dept)	Mar. 1 to Apr. 15	July 10 to 20	Custer	Wetmore	J. W. Coleman	
	3024	Common White	Spring	July 15 to 30	New Haven	South Britain	W. L. Mitchell	
	J027	...do	Apr. 21	Aug. 1	New London	Groton	J. J. Capp	
	3028	...do	May 1	Aug. 14	Fairfield	West Cornwall	T. S. Gold	Raised in Conn. a long time.
	3029	White Russian or Common	Apr. 10 to May 1	July 25 to Aug. 10	Fairfield	Green Farms	W. J. Jennings	
Dakota	3030	Wisconsin White	May 24	Sept. 1	Stutsman	Jamestown	J. J. Nichols	
	3031	(?)	March, early	Last of July	Turner	Swan Lake	S. Frye Andrews	
	3034	Common White	Apr. 19	Aug. 1	Lincoln	Worthing	W. H. Leverett	
	3035	White Russian	May 15	Aug. 15	Cass	Fargo	A. Zenert	Seed years ago from Department, 1881.
	3036	White Australian	Apr. 1	July 15	Bon Homme	Tyndall		
Delaware	3038	Common White	Mar. 22	July 18	New Castle	Red Lion	Samuel Silver	
Florida	3041	Red Rust Proof	December	April to May	Talladega	Tallaha	J. W. Le Feinster	
	3012	Rust Proof	December	May	Columbia	Mikesville	J. R. Liter	
	3043	Major Britton	Dec. 15 to Jan. 15	May	Jackson	Sneads	Pat. Ham	
	3044	Horn Rust Proof	December	June 1	Tallahassee	Leon	Jno. Bradford	
Georgia	3045	Texas Rust Proof	Jan. 1 to 10	June 6	Madison	Greenville	M. W. Linton	
	3047	North Carolina	February	June 15	Bartow	Cartersville	C. H. Smith	
	3049	Hurnicut	July to Oct	June 1 to July 15	Wilkes	Washington	J. T. Wingfield	
	3049 II	Rust Proof	July to Oct	June 1 to July 15	Wilkes	Washington	J. T. Wingfield	From Department several years ago, 1877 or 1878.
	3049 III	Virginia	July to Oct	June 1 to July 15	Wilkes	Washington	J. T. Wingfield	Do.
	3049 IV	Tennessee	July to Oct	June 1 to July 15	Wilkes	Washington	J. T. Wingfield	Do.
	3050	Rust Proof or HornOat	Oct. 1 to Mar. 10	June 1	Thomas	Cairo	E. F. Richt-r	
Illinois	3052	Red Rust Proof	Oct. 1 to Feb. 1	July	Brooks	Quitman	J. G. McCall	
	3055	Common Black	Mar. to Apr	July 15	Madison	Highland	J. Balsiger	
	3057		...do	July to Aug	Clinton	Carlisle	O. B. Nichols	
	3060		Apr	July 25 to Aug. 10	Will	Crete	J. O. Piependrink	
	3062	Schönen	Apr. 10 to May 1	Aug. 1	Stephenson	Howardsville	A. M. Durkee	Seed from Department.
	3063	Common White	Apr	...do	Ogle	Baileyville	W. B. Derrick	
	3065	White Russian	Early Apr	July 20	McHenry	Crystal Lake	F. Cole	
	3068	Black	Apr. 15	July 15 to 20	Livingston	Cayuga	E. W. Pearson	70 bushels per acre.
	3067	Common Mixed	Early spring		Lee	Dixon	Abram Brown	

29

State	No.	Variety	Sown	Harvested	County	P.O. Address	Correspondent	Remarks
Indiana	3068	Norway and a little White	Apr. 3	July 25	La Salle	Tonica	L. A. Burgess	
	3070	Early White Tobin	Apr. 1 to 10	July 15	Kankakee	Momence	A. L. Miner	
	3075	Black	Apr. 15	July 18	Du Page	Downer's Grove	H. L. Bush	
	3078	Barley	Apr. 10	July 25	Champaign	Homer	W. A. Conkey	36 to 40 pounds to bushel.
	3079	Common White	Apr. 1	do	Bureau	Princeton	D. Knight	
	3084	Russian White	Apr. 14	July 15	Lawrence	Erie	Mortimer Grabb	
	3085	Northern	Feb. to Apr. 1	July 1		Rockport	James Lane	
Iowa	3086	Common	Apr. 20	Aug. 1	Spencer	Goshen	P. F. Nye	
	3089	Common White	Mar. 1 to 25		Elkhart	Chase	J. M. Stanley	
	3094	Common	Mar. 20 to Apr. 15	July 15	Benton	Conway	J. L. Hoor	60 to 90 bushels per acre.
	3097	German	Mar. 25 to Apr. 10	July 25 to Aug. 5	Taylor	Wall Lake	J. H. Hoeling	
	3098	White Russian	Apr. 10 to 15		Sac	Ruthvrn	C. A. Anthony	Raised for 5 to 6 years.
	3101	do	May 1	Aug. 1	Palo Alto	Decorah	M. H. Merrill	
	3104	Schönen	Apr	July 25	Winneshiek	West Union	B. F. Conkey	
	3107	Norway Spring	...do	Aug. 1	Fayette	Bryant	Dan. Conrad	
Kansas	3113				Clinton	Galvo	J. Richey	
Kentucky	3116	Norway	Mar. 15 to 30	June 1	McPherson	Louisa	J. M. Clayton, jr	
	3117	Black	Feb. to Mar	July 15	Lawrence	West Liberty	W. W. Cox	
	3119	Red		June	Morgan	Willisburgh	J. B. Lilzey	
	3122	Michigan White	do	July 10	Washington	Fern Creek	Noah Cartwright	
Louisiana	3126	Rust Proof	Mar. 20	June	Jefferson	Mount Lebanon	W. B. Culbert	
	3127	Red Rust Proof	Oct. 1 to 15	May 15 to 30	Bienville	Homer	A. T. Nelson	
Maine	3131	Common Bush	May 1	Aug. 1	Claiborne	Unity	B. R. Stevens	Imported in 1880.
	3133	English	May 16	Aug. 19	Waldo	North Belgrade	A. E. Faught	
Maryland	3134	White Canada	May 20	Aug. 20	Kennebec	Harrison	A. Moulton	
	3140	White Russian	Mar. last	June 25 to July 30	Cumberland	Frederick	H. C. Brown	Fair average.
Michigan	3141	do	Apr. to May	Sept. 1	Frederick	Oakland	P. Hamill	
	3151	do	Apr. 20	Aug. 1st week	Garrett	Flint	F. H. Rankin	
	3153	Early Probsteer	Apr. 21	Aug. 20	Genesee	Hartland	I. D. Crouse	
	3156	Michigan White	Apr. 26	Aug. 15	Livingston	Berlin	C. W. Witte	
	3158	White Russian	Apr. 24	Aug. 5	Ottawa	Jeddo	Mosen Locke	As from thrasher.
Minnesota	3160	Fine Fellows	Apr. 25 to May 10	July 25 to Aug. 1	Saint Clair	Corunna	S. R. Kelsey	
	3163	Common White	Apr. 17	Aug. 12	Shiawassee	Long Prairie	L. S. Hoadley	
	3166	White Dutch	May, middle	Aug. 22	Todd	Deer Creek	C. F. Mason	
	3168	Common White	May 8	Aug. 20	Otter Tail	Anoka	A. Small	
	3169	White Russian	Apr. 10	Aug. 1	Anoka	Mastorville	C. W. Cushing	
	3170	Minn. White and Black	Apr. 10		Dodge	Minnesota City	O. M. Lord	
	3172	White German	Apr. 15	Aug. 1	Winona	Hastings	R. A. Simmons	
	3175	Common White	Apr. 26	do	Dakota	Willow Creek	E. F. Wilder	
	3176	(?)	May 7	do	Blue Earth	Marion	A. J. Goode	
Mississippi	3179			Aug. 5	Olmsted	Fillmore	G. W. Knight	
	3180	Red	Sept. 15 to Feb. 15	May 15 to June 15	Fillmore	Pittsborough	L. W. Harrelson	
	3181	Red Rust-Proof	Oct. to March	June 1	Calhoun	Chester	R. H. Biggers	
	3182	do	Feb. 15	June 15	Choctaw	Hazlehurst	W. J. Rea	
	3183	do	Oct.		Copiah	Poplar Top	E. R. Hart	
Missouri	3184	do	Nov. 15	May to June	De Soto	Station Creek	C. Welch	
	3185	do	Jan. 15	June 15 to 25	Covington	Raymond	W. J. Crisler	
	3187	Irish White	Apr. 1 to 20	July 15 to 25	Hinds	Macon	M. Mahorner	
	3188	Black	Mar. 1st week	July, 2d week	Noxubee	Langdon	R. Buckham	
	3190	White	Apr.	Aug.	Atchison	Fayetteville	W. B. Ames	
	3191				Johnson		Merritt Young	
					Putnam			

30

Sources of specimens of oats—Continued.

State.	Serial No.	Name.	Sown.	Harvested.	County.	Post-office.	Sender.	Remarks.
Montana	3196	Minnesota	Apr. 1	Sept. 1	Meagher	Canton	J. G. Pickering	
	3197	Common White	May 5	do	Gallatin	Bozeman	W. Flannery	
Nebraska	3198	Yellow Russian	Apr. 1	July 10	Antelope	Neligh	F. H. Trowbridge	
	3200	Black and white	Apr. 1st week	Aug. 10	Lancaster	Waverly	W. F. Truell	
Nevada	3205	Poland	Apr. 1	Oct.	Douglas	Genoa	H. F. Dangberg	
New Hampshire	3208	Native	Apr. to May	Aug.	Sullivan	Newport	J. M. Wilmarth	35 pounds per bushel, usually 45; from Centen.
	3209	Russian	May to June	Aug. to Sept.	Coos	Hazen's Mill	L. T. Hazen	
New Jersey	3210	Common White	May 15 to 25	Aug. 1 to 15	Grafton	Blawenburgh	Francis Potter	
	3214	Branch White	Apr. 1	July 20 to 25	Somerset	Morristown	D. C. Voorhees	
	3215	Jersey	Early spring	Aug. 1	Morris		J. R. Runyon	
New Mexico	3218	White and Black	Apr. 20 to May 10	Aug. 20, about	San Miguel	Gallinas Spring	J. E. Whitmore	47 bushels per acre cut green; seed from the West.
New York	3226	Common White	May 8	Aug. 24	Allegany	Nile	J. D. Rogers	
	3228	Western	May 15	Aug. 25	Cattaraugus	Little Valley	J. S. Huntley	
	3230	Common White	Apr. 24	Aug. 8	Delaware	Sidney Plains	I. F. Sherman	
	3231	Native	Apr. 20	Aug. 1	Dutchess	Mount Ross	B. Wilbur	
	3232	Probsteier	May 1 to 15	July 10 to 20	Ontario	Naples	J. M. Anable	
	3233	Marrowfat	Apr. 25	Aug. 1	Otsego	Cooperstown	G. P. Keese	
	5234	Common	Apr. 15 to May 1	Aug. 20 to Sept. 10	Saratoga	Greenfield Centre	R. S. Robinson	
	3235	(?)	Apr. 15	Aug. 1	Schoharie	Schoharie	I. C. Van Tuyl	
	3240				Oneida	Vernona	George Benedict.	Department, 1880.
North Carolina	3243	Mold Ennobled	Apr. 15	Aug. 20	Cayuga	Fleming	H. Tryan	
	3249	Black Prolific	Mar. to Apr	Aug.	Alleghany	Elk Creek	I. W. Landreth	
	3251	Rust Proof	Nov. or Feb.	May or June	Bertie	Windsor	J. B. Martin	
	3253	Red Rust Proof	Sept. 10	June 25	Guilford	New Garden	J. S. Hodgin	
	3255	Early Rust Proof	Aug. to Sept	May 15	Union	Monroe	H. M. Houston	
	3256	Winter	Sept	June	Rockingham	Ruffin	T. L. Rawley	
	3257	Red Rust Proof	do	July	Rowan	Salisbury	J. L. Hedrick	
	3260	Sprauly	Apr. 1 to 15	July 5 to 15	Butler	Gano	Joseph Allen	
	3261	(?)	Apr. 1	Aug. 1	Fulton	Wauseon	J. D. Aldrich	
Ohio	3262	Welcome	Apr. 11 to May 1	July 20 to Aug. 10	Holmes	Black Creek	W. H. Hall	
	8267	Yellow Ohio	Apr. 1	July 15 to 30	Richland	Mansfield	O. F. Stewart	
	3268	White German	Apr. 15	July 24	Seneca	Tiffin	John Seitz	
	3269	Common White	Apr. 10	July 19	Wood	Merrill	Andrew Welton	
	3270	do	Mar. to Apr.	Aug. 1	Williams	Bryan	S. B. McKelvy	
	3271	do			Warren	Lebanon	D. P. Egbert	
Oregon	3272	Schanen	Apr. 15	July 15	Wayne	Apple Creek	L. C. Reichenbach	
	3275	White Russian	Apr. 1	Sept. 1	Baker	Baker City	T. Smith	
	3277	Hopkin	Feb. to May	July to Aug	Linn	Albany	G. F. Crawford	
Pennsylvania	3282	Mixed	Mar. to Apr.	Aug	Union	Lewisburg	J. A. Gundy	
	3285	White Russian	May 11	Aug. 1	Crawford	Conneautville	R. Bolard	

31

South Carolina	3286	Department Seed	Early spring	...do	Butler	...do	Butler	H. I. Serg	
	3286a	Common	do	...do	do	do	do	do	
	3294	Rust Proof	Nov. 10	June 1	Marlborough	Bennettsville	J. H. Parham	
	3295	Red Rust Proof	Nov	May	Charleston	Charleston	G. S. Holmes	
	3296	do	Aug	June	York	Rock Hill	I. Jones	
	3297	do	Sept. to Mar	May to June	Orangeburg	Orangeburg	A. M. Salley	
	3298	do	Sept. 1 to Mar. 1	June 1	Lexington	Lexington	S. Corley	
	3299	do	Sept	June	Laurens	Goodriou's Factory	J. S. Wolf	
	3300	do	Sept. 15 to Nov. 1, and Jan. 15 to Feb. 15.	May 10 to 20	Barnwell	Martin	J. C. Brown	Injured by wet weather.
	3301	do	July 20 to Oct. 30, and until Feb. 1	June 10 to 20	Abbeville	Abbeville	J. F. C. Du Pre	Wet.
Tennessee	3302	Winter	Mar. 10	July 1	Wilson	Watertown	W. L. Waters	
	3303	(?)	Aug. and Sept. and at other times.	June and later	Washington	Crookshanks	J. A. Jones	Late sown.
Texas	3304	Rust Proof	Feb. 15 to Apr. 1	June 20 to July 10	Roane	Kingston	J. R. Martin	
	3309	Gaines Winter	Sept. 15	July 1	Bedford	Rover	B. F. Jarrett	
	3310	White Cluster	Nov. 1	May 15	Anderson	Montalba	W. J. Hamleth, sr	
	3311	Georgia Red Rust Proof.	Oct. 1 to Feb. 1	May 20 to June 10	Travis	Austin	W. H. D. Carrington.	
	3313	Red Rust Proof	Oct. to Mar	May 20 to July 1	Hill	Hilleborough	W. R. Turner	
	3314	do	Feb	June 1 to 15	Denton	Denton	J. W. Kenady	
	3315	Southern Rust Proof	Jan. to Feb	do	Collin	Beth	W. G. Matthews	
	3316	Red Rust Proof	Oct. to Mar	May 1 to June 1	Bell		H. J. Chamberlain	
Utah	3317	do	do	May to June	Dallas	Dallas	J. B. Simpson	Average.
	3319	White Somerset	May 10	Sept. 10	Wasatch	Heber	T. Crook	
Vermont	3321	(?)	Apr. 1	Aug	Sevier	Richfield	William Morrison	
	3322	Common White	May 5		Bennington	Manchester	G. G. Burton	
	3323	White Schönen	May 1 to June 20	Aug. 10 to Sept. 20	Windsor	Pomfret	Crosby Miller	
	3324	White Probsteier	May 5	Aug. 18	Washington	Montpelier	A. D. Arms	
	3326	White Australian			Orleans	Irasburg	Z. E. Jameson	Fourth growth from Department seed.
Virginia	3329	Winter	Aug. 15 to Nov. 15	June 10	Loudon	Farmwell	Van Quick	
	3331	Welcome	Mar. 1 to 25	End of July	Mecklenburg	Clarkeville	J. K. Leigh	
	3334	Winter	Sept. 1 to 20	June 20 to 30	Floyd	Floyd C. H	Benjamin Phlegar	
	3335	Centennial	Mar	July	Bedford	Moreb	J. E. Laceaby	
Washington	3337	Common White	Apr. 1 to 20	Aug. to Sept	Amherst	Harris Creek	M. H. Gorland	
West Virginia	3341	Common White	April 7	July 14	Skagit	Lyman	Lyman Everett	
	3345	Canada White	Apr. 15 to May 1	July 25 to Aug. 1	Wayne	Ceredo	Z. D. Randell	
	3346	White Russian	Apr. 1	July 15	Ohio	Roney's Point	T. J. Orr	
	3347	Canada White	March to April	July 15 to Aug. 10	Fayette	Clifty	A. K. McCutcheon	
Wis	3348	White Snrprise	Apr. 26	July 30	Greenbrier	Lewisburg	H. Handley	Two years here.
	3351	(?)			Chippewa	Eagle Point	John Bates	
	3356	German	Apr. 15	Aug. 10	Rock	Fayette	W. R. Phillips	
	3357	White German	Apr. 15	Aug. 20	La Fayette	Fayetteville	S. E. Roberts	
	3360	White Somerset	Apr. 25 to 30	Aug. 1	Fon du Lac	Metomen	E. Reynolds	
	3361				Dodge	Burnett	Hiram Lawyer	

Sources of specimens of oats—Continued.

SUPPLEMENTARY LIST.

State	Serial No.	Name	Sown	Harvested	County	Post-office	Sender	Remarks
Alabama	3363	Rust Proof	Fall or spring	June 1 to 10	Pickens	Carrollton	S. H. Hill	Average.
Arkansas	3366	Red Rust Proof	November	May	Lee	Marianna	J. M. Daggett	
	3368	Arkansas Red			White	Searcy	R. J. Rogers	
California	3374	(?)	January		Solano		G. S. Myers	
	3378	Egyptian	Jan., Feb., Mar	May to June	Monterey	Salinas	J. R. Leese	
	3380	Common White	Dec. to Apr. 1	End of August	Sonoma	Santa Rosa	E. W. Davis	
	3382	Fielder	Feb. 15		Humboldt	Eureka	Fred Axe	
Colorado	3384	White Belgian	May 28	Aug. 15	Saguache	Saguache	Owen Maione	
	3385	White Russian	Apr. 15	do	Pueblo	Pueblo	I. W. Stanton	
	3386				La Plata	Parrott	(?)	
Dakota	3390	Russian			Trail	Caledonia	P. Herbrandson	
	3391	White	May	Second crop	Lawrence	Deadwood	J. Carney	
Florida	3392	Early Egyptian	Dec. to Feb. 15	Apr. 15 to May 20	Jefferson	Monticello	D. H. Bryan	
Georgia	3395	Rust Proof	Jan. 15	Apr. 15 to May 1	Houston	Perry	G. W. Killen	
Iowa	3445				Lyon	Larchwood	J. R. Warren	
Louisiana	3441	Red Rust Proof	Oct. 15 to Feb. 15	May 15 to June 15	Lincoln	Vienna	E. M. Graham	
Michigan	3406	Common White	May 20	Sept. 1	Cheboygan	Cheboygan	Jacob Walton	
Minnesota	3407	Yellow German	Apr. 13	July 17	Wabasha	Wabasha	H. I. Whitmore	
Missouri	3411	Yellow			Cedar	Stockton	J. A. Barron	
Montana	3415	White Russian	May 10 to 20	Sept. 1	Deer Lodge	Deer Lodge City	D. C. Irvine	
New Mexico	3420	White	March late	Sept	Taos	Fernandez de Taos	W. L. McClure	
Ohio	3444		Mar. 1	June to July	Butler	Hamilton	G. H. Shaffer	
South Carolina	3429	Red Rust Proof	Aug. to Sept	Early June	Edgefield	Edgefield C. H	E. L. Geerard	
Texas	3430	do	Spring or fall		Hill	Hillsborough	J. W. Perry	
Washington	3435	Gray Winter	Early spring	Late Sept	Pierce	Tacoma	L. E. Sampson	

Physical properties of oats.

State.	Serial number.	Weight of 100 grains.	Clean grain.	Hulled grain.	Hulls.	Weight per bushel.	Color.
		Grams.	Per cent.	Per cent.	Per cent.	Lbs.	
Maine	3131	2.144	96.02	69.54	30.46	34.7	Light.
Do	3133	2.610	98.22	69.65	30.35	44.2	White.
Do	3134	2.279	97.89	71.68	28.32	30.8	Light.
New Hampshire	3208	2.060	98.04			33.5	Yellow and green.
Do	3209	2.890	85.34	70.88	29.12	40.7	Yellow.
Do	3210	2.465	98.10	72.20	27.80	40.7	Light.
Vermont	3322	2.324	97.27	71.01	28.99	40.2	White.
Do	3323	2.122	93.74	70.98	29.02	36.9	Light.
Do	3324	2.695	93.65	71.39	28.61	37.3	Do.
Do	3326	2.756	95.22	64.72	35.28	43.1	Do.
Connecticut	3024	1.796	97.00	69.25	30.75	37.7	Yellow and green.
Do	3027	1.935	91.90	65.70	31.30	29.5	Light.
Do	3038	2.128	97.97	72.18	27.82	37.6	White.
Do	3029	2.580	96.15	62.63	37.37	37.6	Light brown.
Total		8.439	383.11	269.76	130.24	142.4	
Average		2.810	95.78	67.44	32.56	35.6	
New York	3226	2.342	98.70	66.70	33.30	39.0	Light.
Do	3228	2.663	92.57	73.83	26.17	40.1	Mixed.
Do	3230					38.0	Light.
Do	3231	2.192	95.80	68.20	31.80	33.2	Do.
Do	3232	2.856	96.10	73.50	26.50	42.0	Do.
Do	3233	3.127	98.17	71.49	28.51	41.8	Do.
Do	3234	2.039	99.14	70.82	29.18	37.3	White.
Do	3245	2.921	80.30	73.24	26.76	44.1	Brown.
Do	3243	2.430	95.81	70.20	29.80	41.9	Do.
New Jersey	3214	2.709	98.80	75.10	24.90	41.4	White.
Do	3215	2.033	98.20	70.40	29.60	31.7	Light.
Pennsylvania	3282	2.207	96.44	69.65	30.35	32.5	Do.
Do	3285	2.617	96.04	69.04	30.96	38.1	Do.
Do	3280	3.010	94.15	71.34	28.66	43.7	White.
Do	3286¹	2.910	81.44	64.18	35.82	37.8	Light.
Ohio	3260	2.248	99.30	73.33	26.67	39.9	White.
Do	3261	2.130	87.74	74.95	25.05	41.0	Light.
Do	3262	2.670	96.84	60.83	39.17	40.0	Do.
Do	3267	2.722	95.31	72.07	27.93	39.9	Do.
Do	3268	2.224	98.30	74.62	25.38	40.0	Do.
Do	3269	2.010	95.56	69.08	30.92	37.8	Yellow and green.
Do	3270	2.260	99.21	73.54	26.46	40.1	Light.
Do	3271	2.012	99.15	73.31	26.69		
Do	3444	2.025	96.36	71.25	28.75		
Michigan	3151	2.430	94.59	74.30	25.70	41.1	Light.
Do	3153	2.400	94.25	72.16	27.84	43.6	White.
Do	3156	2.864	97.58	72.41	27.59	42.8	Light.
Do	3158	2.904	97.09	70.91	29.09	43.7	White.
Do	310	2.507	93.58	72.47	27.53	39.4	Light.
Do	3406	3.237	94.25	71.62	28.38	43.2	White.
Indiana	3084	2.414	90.65	70.60	29.31	35.3	Do.
Do	3086	2.086	82.73	73.40	26.60	39.4	Light.
Do	3089	2.060	97.71	71.92	28.08	35.4	Do.
Illinois	3055		96.37	74.75	25.25	40.7	Mixed.
Do	3060	2.370		66.58	33.42	41.5	White.
Do	3062	2.030	99.52	69.53	30.47	36.2	Light.
Do	3063	1.980	97.89	72.74	27.26	37.1	Light brown.
Do	3065	2.517	98.27	70.97	29.03	38.6	Light.
Do	3066	2.512	93.30	75.85	24.15	40.5	Brown.
Do	3067	2.014	98.35	70.46	29.54	38.8	Mixed.
Do	3068	3.025	98.93	74.97	25.03	41.5	Do.
Do	3068¹		95.69	72.32	27.68		
Wisconsin	3357	2.920	95.24	70.53	29.47	43.7	Light.
Do	3353	2.430	96.53	68.99	31.01	39.7	Mixed.
Do	3357	2.377	97.10	70.03	29.97	34.9	White.
Do	3360	2.580	89.63	73.25	26.75	35.6	Do.
Do	3361	2.109	95.55	71.05	28.95	37.1	Do.
Minnesota	3166	2.180	97.84	69.27	30.73	35.4	Light brown.
Do	3168	2.038	98.10	73.50	26.50	42.0	White.
Do	3169	2.678	99.39	69.88	30.12	40.2	Do.
Do	3170	2.170	93.40	73.00	27.00	38.3	Light.
Do	3172	2.770		72.62	27.38	48.4	White.
Do	3175	2.046	91.80	72.40	27.60	39.8	Mixed.
Do	3175¹	2.075	93.72	72.91	27.09	38.1	Do.
Do	3176	2.610	98.14	69.60	30.40	40.5	White.
Do	3179	2.162	96.10	71.90	28.10	39.6	Light.
Iowa	3094	1.924	97.53	67.31	32.69	33.5	Do.
Do	3097	2.402	94.55	73.43	26.57	40.6	White.
Do	3098	2.253	97.07	74.78	25.22		
Do	3101	2.413	95.94	71.87	28.13	42.1	Mixed.
Do	3104	2.172	97.16	70.07	29.93	34.9	Light.
Do	3107	2.308	97.67	72.34	27.66	37.1	Brown.

13734—No. 9——3

Physical properties of oats—Continued.

State.	Serial number.	Weight of 100 grains.	Clean grain.	Hulled grain.	Hulls.	Weight per bushel.	Color.
		Grams.	Per cent.	Per cent.	Per cent.	Pounds.	
Missouri	3190	2.016	97.84	71.45	28.55	36.7	Mixed.
Do	3191	1.630	97.70	68.60	31.40		
Do	3411	1.956	98.85	69.28	30.72	38.8	Yellow.
Nebraska	3198	2.194	99.00	73.20	26.80	30.5	Do.
Do	3200	1.582	97.20	68.30	31.70	30.2	Mixed.
Do	3200¹	1.512	97.40	68.79	31.21	29.7	Do.
Dakota	3030	2.057	96.43	67.90	32.10	40.2	White.
Do	3035	2.367	92.04	72.39	27.61	44.7	Yellow.
Do	3036	2.957	96.12	62.20	37.80	48.6	Light.
Do	3390	2.844	92.33	73.16	26.84	44.3	Do.
Do	3391	2.372	87.70	55.37	44.63	38.8	White.
Montana	3196	2.528	94.49	70.10	29.90	45.0	White and bro
Do	3197	2.010	90.16	69.15	30.85	45.4	White.
Do	3415	2.691	88.54	72.36	27.64	39.5	Yellow.
Maryland	3140	1.850	94.86	71.70	28.30	35.0	Light.
Do	3141	2.637	91.65	71.36	28.64	40.0	Do.
Delaware	3038	1.976	98.04	69.59	30.41		
Virginia	3331	2.720	93.00	72.40	27.60	39.0	Brown.
Do	3334	2.771	96.92	59.00	41.00	41.4	White.
Do	3335	2.480	94.09	64.29	35.71	35.5	Light.
Do	3337					40.8	White.
West Virginia	3345	1.872	97.19	71.26	28.74	37.4	Do.
Do	3346	3.386	96.55	67.59	32.41	38.3	Light.
Do	3347	1.969	93.55	64.48	35.52	38.5	Do.
Do	3348	2.773	96.45	62.60	37.40	36.4	Light brown.
North Carolina	3249	2.060	93.94	70.50	29.50	47.8	Brown.
Do	3251	1.834	97.10	70.30	29.70	36.4	Mixed.
Do	3253	3.362	94.30	68.70	31.30	37.2	Brown.
Do	3255	2.470	88.84	70.44	29.56	39.5	Black.
Do	3256	2.314	96.20	73.34	26.66	41.1	Light brown.
Do	3257	2.935	96.77	68.95	31.05	36.6	Brown.
South Carolina	3295	3.039	98.51	69.95	30.05	39.5	Do.
Do	3296	2.823	93.76	67.24	32.76	38.5	Do.
Do	3297	2.055	96.22	68.65	31.35	35.7	Light brown.
Do	3298	2.052	96.90	68.72	31.28	35.9	Yellow.
Do	3299	2.831	94.01	68.48	31.52		
Do	3300	3.176	97.59	71.20	28.80	41.5	Brown.
Do	3301	2.981	93.78	73.33	26.67	37.8	Light brown.
Do	3429	3.179	97.17	68.61	31.39	39.8	Brown.
Kentucky	3116	2.270	98.52	72.70	27.30		
Do	3117	1.908	98.23	71.49	28.51	33.3	Mixed.
Do	3119	2.807	92.22	68.51	31.49	31.9	Brown.
Do	3122	1.860	90.56	67.27	32.73	29.9	Light.
Tennessee	3302	1.897	99.20	68.24	31.76	31.4	Brown.
Do	3303	2.378	91.39	68.75	31.25	38.3	Do.
Do	3304	2.920	97.11	67.66	32.34	35.5	Do.
Do	3309	2.160	94.86	57.01	42.99	39.9	Do.
Georgia	3047	2.236	98.44	70.95	29.05	33.4	Light.
Do	3049	3.255	97.39	68.88	31.12		
Do	3049¹	2.388	91.34	71.18	28.82		
Do	3049²		91.64	73.52	26.48		
Do	3050	2.000	96.42	65.17	34.83	31.4	Brown.
Do	3052	2.830	90.99	67.78	32.22	32.0	Do.
Do	3395	2.334	94.29	62.47	37.53	29.6	Do.
Florida	3041	2.880	99.69	67.13	32.87	31.5	Brown.
Do	3043	2.018	98.70	68.61	31.39	26.9	Yellow.
Do	3044	2.966	93.95	71.69	28.31	31.0	Brown
Do	3045	2.531	98.26	69.40	30.60	31.5	Do.
Do	3392	2.315	98.33	67.85	32.15	24.2	Yellow.
Alabama	3001	2.924	97.36			32.0	Brown.
Do	3002	3.068	97.23	68.34	31.66	24.7	Do.
Do	3007	2.498	94.86	66.48	33.52	32.4	Do.
Do	3008	3.127	94.10	69.39	30.61	36.0	Do.
Do	3363	3.100	98.81	68.47	31.53	33.3	Do.
Mississippi	3181	3.034	96.50	69.50	30.50	34.5	Do.
Do	3183	2.950	96.50	67.80	32.20	34.8	Do.
Do	3184	2.792	91.20	73.69	26.31	30.1	Do.
Do	3185	2.113	70.00	74.60	25.40	38.2	Do.
Do	3187	2.808	97.80	67.00	33.00	34.4	Do.
Louisiana	3126	2.993	99.20	69.34	30.66	33.0	Do.
Do	3127	2.775	90.03	68.19	31.81	35.3	Do.
Do	3441	3.104	95.65	72.10	27.84	42.6	Do.
Arkansas	3012					36.5	Do.
Do	3368	2.760	97.08	64.10	35.90	33.8	Do.
Texas	3310	3.055	98.62	70.18	29.82	31.4	Yellow.
Do	3311	2.491	96.48	71.79	28.21	34.8	Brown.
Do	3313	2.920	96.37	73.51	26.49	34.8	Do.
Do	3314	2.841	98.73	69.78	30.22	37.6	Do.

Physical properties of oats—Continued.

State.	Serial number.	Weight of 100 grains.	Clean grain.	Hulled grain.	Hulls.	Weight per bushel.	Color.
		Grams.	*Per cent.*	*Per cent.*	*Per cent.*	*Pounds.*	
Texas	3315	3.030	93.86	70.74	29.26	41.6	Brown.
Do	3316	2.903	92.90	71.22	28.78	37.3	Do.
Do	3317	3.169	96.76	72.78	27.22	39.7	Do.
Do	3430	2.981	96.64	72.49	27.51	34.6	Do.
Colorado	3020	2.958	86.61	69.76	30.24	48.8	White.
Do	3021	2.247	...	69.32	30.68	42.4	Light.
Do	3385	2.163	93.70	70.31	29.69	38.6	White.
Utah	3319	2.560	90.72	61.17	38.83	43.6	White.
Nevada	3205	2.019	93.05	66.01	33.99	41.1	White.
New Mexico	3218	2.462	97.67	73.21	26.79	43.9	Brown.
Do	3420	...	...	...	...	39.6	Mixed.
Washington Territory	3341	3.255	98.48	72.91	27.09	43.5	White.
Do	3435	3.148	97.16	79.28	20.72	43.2	Light brown.
Oregon	3275	2.772	96.85	73.09	26.91	46.9	White.
Do	3277	3.786	97.09	59.15	40.85	43.3	Do.

From the preceding tables it appears that in the North white (including in this color yellow), black and white, and black oats are principally sown, while in the South varieties of the red rust proof are almost entirely grown.

In the North the crop is put in in April or May and harvested in July or August. In the South it is sown from November to January and harvested in May or June.

The difference in appearance is marked between the crops of these two sections of the country. The Southern oats are large, light, awned varieties, of reddish brown color, with inflated husks not nearly filled by the kernel. The Northern grain is smaller, more compact, not often awned, and with the husk in the better samples well filled out.

Notwithstanding these characteristics, we learn from averages of the results that the size and weight of the Southern clean kernel is rather larger than the Northern. Its fluffy husk, however, makes them lighter oats in weight per bushel.

The averages have been calculated for various sections as follows: The Northern States include all north of Maryland and Kentucky, together with Missouri, Montana, and Dakota; the Southern, all south of these; and the Pacific slope, Colorado, Nevada, New Mexico, Washington Territory, Oregon, and Utah; the Atlantic slope consists of the States east of the Ohio river and the Gulf; the Western States, of those west of this line, excepting those on the Pacific slope. The same classification is preserved with the other cereals.

Average physical properties of oats.

State.	Number of specimens.	Weight of 100 kernels.	Clean grain.	Hulled grain.	Hulls.	Weight per bushel.
			Per cent.	Per cent.	Per cent.	Lbs.
United States	166	2.507	95.00	69.97	30.03	37.2
Northern States	90	2.290	95.63	70.60	29.30	38.0
Southern States	66	2.028	94.18	69.08	30.92	34.5
Pacific Slope	20	2.737	94.93	69.52	30.48	43.2
Atlantic Slope	58	2.523	95.37	69.00	30.31	37.0
Western States	61	2.339	95.82	72.20	27.80	37.8
Maine	3	2.344	97.38	70.29	29.71	38.6
New Hampshire	3	2.472	93.83	71.54	28.46	38.3
Vermont	4	2.474	94.97	69.52	30.48	39.4
Connecticut	4	2.110	95.78	67.44	32.56	35.6
Rhode Island	1	3.029	97.16	67.27	32.73	32.3
New York	8	2.571	95.32	71.00	29.00	39.8
New Jersey	2	2.371	98.50	72.75	27.25	36.6
Pennsylvania	4	2.686	92.24	68.55	31.45	38.0
Ohio	9	2.256	96.42	71.44	28.56	39.8
Michigan	6	2.767	96.22	72.31	27.69	42.3
Indiana	3	2.188	93.36	72.00	28.00	36.7
Illinois	9	2.350	97.21	72.02	27.98	39.4
Wisconsin	5	2.487	94.81	70.77	29.23	30.0
Minnesota	9	2.416	96.09	71.67	28.33	43.6
Iowa	6	2.245	96.90	71.63	28.37	38.4
Missouri	3	1.867	98.13	69.78	30.22	37.8
Nebraska	3	1.763	97.87	70.10	29.90	33.1
Dakota	5	2.519	92.92	66.20	33.80	43.3
Montana	3	2.410	91.06	70.54	29.46	30.0
Maryland	2	2.244	93.26	71.53	28.47	37.5
Delaware	1	1.976	98.04	69.69	30.41	
Virginia	3	2.657	94.67	65.23	34.77	39.2
West Virginia	4	2.500	95.94	66.48	33.52	39.2
North Carolina	6	2.496	94.52	70.37	29.63	39.8
South Carolina	8	2.707	95.99	69.52	30.48	38.4
Kentucky	4	2.249	94.88	69.99	30.01	31.7
Tennessee	4	2.089	95.66	65.42	34.58	30.3
Georgia	7	2.619	93.39	68.56	31.44	31.6
Florida	5	2.542	97.79	68.94	31.06	29.0
Alabama	5	2.961	96.47	68.17	31.83	31.7
Mississippi	5	2.751	90.40	70.52	29.48	34.4
Louisiana	3	2.957	94.99	69.90	30.10	36.9
Arkansas	1	2.760	97.08	64.10	35.90	35.2
Colorado	5	2.442	90.16	69.80	30.21	43.3
Texas	8	2.924	96.29	71.56	28.44	36.5
Utah	1	2.560	90.72	61.17	38.83	43.6
Nevada	1	2.019	95.05	66.01	33.99	41.1
New Mexico	1	2.462	97.67	73.21	26.79	41.8
Washington Territory	2	3.602	98.34	76.10	23.90	43.4
Oregon	2	3.279	96.97	66.12	33.88	45.1

Oats having the husk (pallets and at times glumes) adherent is necessarily lighter than wheat in weight per hundred grains. The heaviest is from the Pacific slope, and the South ranks next, owing, as has been said, to its large size. In weight per bushel, however, the fluffy husk of the Southern grain makes it the lowest in the country, while the Pacific slope retains the highest weight per bushel, as also size and weight per 100, showing it to have a plump, well-filled grain.

The average for the country, 37.2 pounds, appears rather high in comparison with the most common legal weight, 32 pounds, but, as in the case of wheat, the determinations have been proved correct for the specimens examined, and are not mere estimates. The samples are, too, apparently fair averages, as the figures giving percentages of clean grain in the specimens as received show that no particular pains was taken to prepare them for exhibition before reaching us. The range with this cereal is larger than with any other. The extremes in weight per 100 grains were, serial No. 3200, the lightest, from Nebraska, 1.582 grams, and serial No. 3277, from Oregon, the heaviest, 3.786 grams. Cleanliness varied from 99.8 per cent. to 70.0 per cent., but of course had nothing to do with locality. The heaviest weight per bushel was found in specimens from Colorado, serial No. 3020, and Dakota, serial No. 3036, weighing 48.8 and 48.6 pounds. The lightest were from Alabama, serial No. 3002, and from Florida, serial No. 3043, 24.7 and 26.9 pounds, respectively.

In milling oats the relation of kernel to waste is about one-half. Our results show that the relation of kernel to husk averages for the whole country 7 to 3, those from the Western States being a little less husky, and those from the South considerably more so. It is, however, the inflated nature of the husk in the Southern grain and the fact that the glumes or outer husk is often adherent that affects the weight per bushel more than the slightly larger proportion.

The extremes found were 79.28 per cent. of kernel in a specimen from Washington Territory, serial No. 3435, and 55.37 per cent. in one from Dakota, serial No. 3391. Washington and Oregon sustain their reputation for fine looking grain, while the small proportion of kernel in the Dakota specimen is due entirely to cutting before it was quite ripened. It is hardly a fair example, other specimens from the Territory reaching over 70.0 per cent. of kernel.

In weight per bushel the warm climate of the South so affects the form of the grain as to lower its average 2.7 pounds. This is hardly as large as would be expected, and leads to the conclusion that the climate has a greater effect than some other characteristics. One of these is yield, which, from an average of 30 bushels in the North, falls to about 10 in the South, and, as has been said, the color and shape of the grain is much changed.

CHEMICAL COMPOSITION.

In examining the physical relations of the specimens they were separated into kernel and husk, and for several reasons they were separately submitted to analysis with, as it appears, results furnishing much more information than would otherwise have been obtained. Corn, wheat, and rye were analyzed in the clean kernel, and comparison is more readily made between them and oats. The variations, independent of the proportion of husk, are easily arrived at, and since the analysis of the hull and its relative amount are given it is easy to calculate for any specimen its composition as it would be used for feed.

The data obtained are here presented, together with averages derived therefrom:

Composition of American oats, arranged by States.

State.	Serial No.	Water.	Ash.	Oil.	Carbohydrates.	Fiber.	Albuminoids.	Nitrogen.
		Pr. ct.	Pr. ct.	Pr. ct.	Pr. ct.	Pr. ct.	Pr. ct.	Pr. ct.
Maine	3131	7.20	1.80	9.03	66.65	1.67	13.65	2.18
	3133	7.26	2.29	8.54	66.41	1.85	13.65	2.18
	3134	7.10	1.64	8.08	66.15	1.80	15.23	2.44
New Hampshire	3208	7.20	2.13	8.41	65.11	1.40	15.75	2.52
	3209	7.02	2.31	8.46	66.10	1.23	14.88	2.38
	3210	6.95	2.45	8.21	64.61	1.33	16.45	2.63
Vermont	3322	7.60	2.09	8.65	65.76	1.20	14.70	2.35
	3323	7.00	2.08	8.12	64.18	1.46	18.20	2.91
	3324	6.15	1.70	8.30	67.85	1.30	14.70	2.35
	3326	6.58	2.26	7.15	67.81	1.42	14.88	2.38
Connecticut	3024	6.24	2.30	7.54	67.56	1.48	14.88	2.38
	3027	6.52	2.20	8.23	60.27	1.53	12.25	1.96
	3028	7.62	2.25	8.72	67.46	1.35	12.60	2.02
	3029	5.77	2.46	7.74	67.99	1.51	14.53	2.32
Rhode Island	3204	7.52	2.02	8.71	68.66	1.01	12.08	1.93
New York	3226	7.33	2.09	8.13	69.07	1.48	11.90	1.90
	3228	7.20	2.15	7.15	67.56	1.22	14.35	2.30
	3230	7.50	2.20	8.46	66.01	1.48	14.35	2.30
	3231	7.46	2.43	8.01	64.81	1.54	15.75	2.52
	3232	7.20	2.37	7.13	66.24	1.31	15.75	2.52
	3233	7.58	2.23	7.79	67.50	1.89	12.95	2.07
	3234	9.24	1.93	9.63	64.88	1.19	13.13	2.10
	3235	7.28	1.78	8.52	67.74	1.20	13.48	2.18
	3243	6.34	2.03	6.98	65.02	1.60	18.03	2.88
New Jersey	3214	7.26	2.34	6.86	67.18	1.31	15.05	2.41
	3215	7.57	2.24	7.42	65.93	1.26	15.58	2.49
Pennsylvania	3282	6.73	2.64	8.41	62.91	1.43	17.88	2.85
	3285	6.86	2.08	8.08	67.82	.98	14.18	2.27
	3286	7.88	2.30	7.90	67.02	1.25	13.65	2.18
	3286	6.92	2.40	7.62	65.67	1.64	15.75	2.52
Ohio	3260	7.04	2.43	7.75	66.29	1.23	15.26	2.44
	3261	7.00	1.92	8.01	64.11	1.46	17.50	2.80
	3262	6.78	2.07	7.40	63.21	1.10	19.44	3.11
	3267	6.45	1.96	8.67	64.80	.97	17.15	2.74
	3268	6.76	2.65	8.67	64.58	1.26	16.10	2.58
	3269	6.83	2.12	8.85	66.84	1.18	14.18	2.27
	3270	6.77	2.20	8.88	66.37	1.25	14.53	2.32
	3271	6.71	2.40	8.34	66.13	1.19	15.23	2.44
	3444	6.55	2.50	8.33	66.19	1.03	15.40	2.46
Michigan	3151	7.95	2.10	8.42	65.55	1.10	14.88	2.38
	3153	6.67	2.94	7.42	65.43	1.26	16.28	2.60
	3156	6.89	2.57	7.40	68.15	1.16	13.83	2.21
	3158	7.44	2.06	7.48	68.31	1.23	13.48	2.16
	3160	7.10	2.33	7.52	67.69	1.18	14.18	2.27
	3406	6.60	2.12	8.17	70.50	1.23	11.38	1.82
Indiana	3084	8.15	1.65	7.40	66.25	1.15	15.40	2.46
	3086	7.20	2.13	8.23	65.09	1.16	16.10	2.58
	3089	8.72	1.98	7.83	65.72	1.40	14.35	2.30
Illinois	3055	6.18	2.66	7.22	68.38	1.38	14.18	2.27
	3060	5.88	2.16	7.59	68.82	1.55	14.00	2.24
	3062	7.00	2.64	7.09	67.89	1.55	13.83	2.21
	3063	5.41	2.24	8.12	67.95	1.40	14.88	2.38
	3065	6.29	2.06	8.09	66.53	1.80	15.23	2.44
	3066	5.28	2.49	7.23	67.27	1.08	15.75	2.52
	3067	6.11	2.42	7.70	68.34	1.43	14.00	2.24
	3068	6.60	2.15	7.85	67.62	1.43	14.35	2.30
	3068	6.92	2.37	7.82	66.41	1.43	15.05	2.41
Wisconsin	3351	6.82	2.30	7.35	68.14	1.56	13.83	9.21
	3353	7.84	2.28	7.82	68.90	1.26	11.90	1.90
	3357	6.86	2.02	7.55	69.58	1.30	12.60	2.02
	3360	7.12	1.45	7.32	67.83	1.75	14.53	2.32
	3361	7.72	2.25	7.21	67.82	1.48	13.48	2.16
Minnesota	3166	6.69	2.15	8.24	69.36	1.30	12.25	1.96
	3168	7.15	2.45	8.70	66.35	1.17	14.18	2.27
	3169	7.63	2.35	7.30	69.11	1.01	12.60	2.02
	3170	6.88	2.23	7.90	66.26	1.33	15.40	2.46
	3172	8.07	2.18	7.97	68.09	1.09	12.60	2.02
	3175	7.07	2.38	7.73	67.52	1.47	13.83	2.21
	3175	6.95	2.10	7.88	67.75	1.84	13.48	2.16
	3176	6.82	2.38	7.61	71.22	1.29	10.68	1.71
	3179	7.15	2.19	7.90	69.32	1.19	12.25	1.96
Iowa	3004	6.46	1.92	6.94	65.50	1.50	17.68	2.86
	3007	6.40	2.07	7.75	69.44	1.04	13.30	2.13
	3098	7.38	2.61	9.60	65.15	1.08	14.18	2.27

Composition of American oats, asranged by States—Continued.

State.	Serial No.	Water.	Ash.	Oil.	Carbohydrates.	Fiber.	Albuminoids.	Nitrogen.
		Pr. ct.	Pr. ct.	Pr. ct.	Pr. ct.	Pr. ct.	Pr. ct.	Pr. ct.
Iowa	3101	6.56	2.06	7.88	68.66	1.71	13.13	2.10
	3104	7.66	.84	7.96	67.06	1.60	14.88	2.38
	3107	7.98	2.32	7.93	65.20	1.60	14.88	2.38
	3445	6.65	2.35	8.07	66.06	1.47	15.40	2.46
Missouri	3190	6.81	2.07	8.95	67.42	1.45	13.30	2.13
	3191	7.58	2.07	8.34	66.33	1.50	14.18	2.27
	3411	6.95	1.60	7.77	62.86	1.57	19.25	3.08
Nebraska	3198	8.03	2.02	6.91	66.81	1.35	14.88	2.38
	3200	6.90	2.21	8.32	66.72	1.85	14.00	2.24
	3200	7.32	2.24	8.72	66.39	1.33	14.00	2.24
Dakota	3030	6.12	2.27	8.27	68.67	1.37	13.30	2.13
	3035	6.38	2.29	8.12	67.86	1.35	14.06	2.24
	3036	5.00	2.40	7.00	66.11	1.03	17.50	2.80
	3390	6.54	2.08	7.94	68.16	1.10	14.18	2.27
	3391	8.75	2.15	9.47	66.17	1.56	11.90	1.90
Montana	3196	7.10	2.18	8.79	66.39	1.54	14.00	2.24
	3197	7.10	2.26	9.72	67.87	1.32	11.73	1.88
	3415	11.13	2.15	9.03	64.42	1.02	12.25	1.96
Maryland	3140	6.32	2.31	8.48	65.59	1.55	15.75	2.52
	3141	7.70	2.40	7.35	67.19	1.36	14.00	2.24
Delaware	3038	5.94	2.27	7.75	66.09	1.35	16.60	2.66
Virginia	3331	6.73	2.45	9.30	66.76	1.42	13.65	2.18
	3334	6.43	2.53	7.25	66.20	1.14	16.45	2.63
	3335	6.13	2.35	8.58	66.55	1.51	14.88	2.38
	3337	7.24	2.80	6.50	64.58	1.90	16.98	2.72
West Virginia	3345	6.45	2.32	8.65	64.94	1.54	16.10	2.58
	3346	7.10	2.14	7.34	65.63	1.34	16.45	2.63
	3347	6.45	2.10	7.42	63.84	1.37	18.73	3.00
	3348	6.57	2.50	6.62	65.03	1.60	17.68	2.86
North Carolina	3249	7.78	2.02	7.32	71.91	1.87	9.10	1.46
	3251	6.34	2.56	8.68	66.00	1.54	14.88	2.38
	3253	6.82	2.19	8.64	67.59	1.11	13.65	2.18
	3255	6.77	1.83	6.92	69.18	2.00	13.30	2.13
	3256	6.77	1.80	9.77	67.08	1.63	12.95	2.07
	3257	6.58	1.98	8.26	67.91	1.62	13.65	2.18
South Carolina	3295	6.16	2.18	8.65	68.50	1.03	13.48	2.16
	3296	6.94	1.76	9.51	68.40	1.14	12.25	1.96
	3297	7.90	1.86	7.15	69.04	.92	13.13	2.10
	3298	7.08	1.93	8.13	68.20	1.01	13.65	2.18
	3299	6.62	1.74	9.55	67.31	1.13	13.65	2.18
	3300	7.02	2.06	8.59	68.15	.88	13.30	2.13
	3301	7.40	2.16	7.97	68.09	.90	13.48	2.16
	3429	7.40	3.00	8.31	67.90	.96	12.43	1.99
Kentucky	3116	8.03	2.02	7.36	65.22	1.62	15.75	2.52
	3117	7.25	1.95	9.39	65.33	2.08	14.00	2.24
	3119	6.72	2.43	6.90	68.41	1.19	14.35	2.30
	3122	7.37	2.00	7.55	64.92	2.06	16.10	2.58
Tennessee	3302	6.80	2.20	7.59	66.13	1.53	15.75	2.52
	3303	6.66	1.88	8.03	68.36	1.34	13.13	2.10
	3304	6.81	2.74	7.07	67.63	1.40	14.35	2.30
	3399	6.96	2.04	9.07	67.21	1.42	13.30	2.13
Georgia	3047	6.14	3.07	8.44	68.12	1.28	12.95	2.07
	3049	7.24	1.78	8.03	67.45	1.12	13.48	2.16
	3049	4.88	2.23	8.92	68.17	.92	14.88	2.38
	3049	7.28	1.93	7.72	65.92	1.22	15.93	2.55
	3049	6.57	2.02	8.04	67.23	1.36	14.18	2.27
	3050	4.85	1.85	8.03	69.28	1.81	14.18	2.27
	3052	5.82	2.30	7.26	70.40	1.44	12.78	2.04
	3305	6.40	2.25	10.38	64.61	1.66	14.70	2.35
Florida	3041	5.83	2.52	7.68	68.93	1.56	13.48	2.16
	3043	6.09	1.60	8.32	66.50	1.39	16.10	2.58
	3044	6.32	2.25	7.68	68.32	.90	14.53	2.32
	3045	5.93	2.38	8.25	68.93	1.56	12.95	2.07
	3392	5.99	1.05	10.51	66.57	1.45	13.83	2.21
Alabama	3001	5.11	2.30	8.20	68.65	1.04	14.70	2.35
	3002	8.59	1.80	8.98	66.20	1.20	15.23	2.44
	3007	6.28	1.55	8.95	66.92	1.07	15.23	2.44
	3008	7.24	2.10	7.89	68.29	1.00	13.48	2.16
	3363	6.78	1.94	8.08	67.68	1.52	14.00	2.24
Mississippi	3181	7.53	1.07	7.67	68.49	1.21	13.13	2.10
	3183	7.13	2.14	7.61	67.99	1.13	14.00	2.24
	3184	8.10	1.69	8.06	66.16	1.29	14.70	2.35
	3185	7.05	2.10	7.81	67.32	1.54	14.18	2.27
	3187	7.21	1.95	8.15	67.46	1.23	14.00	2.24

Composition of American oats, arranged by States—Continued.

State.	Serial No.	Water.	Ash.	Oil.	Carbohydrates.	Fiber.	Albuminoids.	Nitrogen.
		Per ct.	P. ct.	Per ct.	Per ct.	P. ct.	Per ct.	P. ct.
Louisiana	3126	9.50	2.20	8.18	64.99	1.13	14.00	2.24
	3127	8.00	2.10	7.83	67.72	1.05	13.30	2.13
	3441	6.85	2.10	8.25	66.03	1.34	14.53	2.32
Arkansas	3012	4.67	2.10	8.12	69.35	1.03	13.83	2.21
	3368	6.94	2.14	7.71	65.83	1.63	15.75	2.52
Texas	3310	7.08	1.74	8.09	68.07	1.12	13.30	2.13
	3311	6.92	2.08	11.20	65.24	1.55	12.95	2.07
	3313	8.57	2.15	9.06	62.82	1.65	15.75	2.52
	3314	6.70	1.86	8.80	67.26	1.03	14.35	2.30
	3315	7.14	2.26	8.75	67.58	1.14	13.13	2.10
	3316	6.80	1.82	8.08	68.02	1.20	13.48	2.16
	3317	6.95	2.10	8.19	68.63	.83	13.30	2.13
	3130	7.10	2.30	7.45	67.81	1.16	14.18	2.27
Colorado	3020	4.80	2.08	7.27	66.82	1.00	18.03	2.88
	3021	5.08	2.40	8.67	68.98	1.14	13.13	2.10
	3385	6.56	2.23	7.67	65.75	1.10	16.63	2.66
	3583	7.20	2.45	7.59	64.46	1.17	13.13	2.10
Utah	3319	6.05	2.37	8.17	69.71	1.62	12.08	1.93
	3321	7.30	2.40	8.81	66.89	1.82	12.78	2.04
Nevada	3205	6.80	2.27	9.72	66.21	1.17	13.83	2.21
New Mexico	3218	6.61	2.12	9.89	66.02	1.88	13.48	2.16
	3420	7.05	2.50	9.43	66.30	1.59	13.13	2.10
Washington	3341	7.08	1.79	7.99	71.56	1.95	9.63	1.54
	3435	6.55	1.55	10.57	68.36	1.07	11.90	1.90
Oregon	3275	6.72	2.28	8.89	68.73	1.48	11.90	1.90
	3277	7.01	2.42	7.87	66.80	2.07	13.83	2.21
California	3016	7.95	1.93	8.63	64.33	1.83	13.13	2.10
	3374	7.22	1.58	9.67	67.94	1.86	11.73	1.88
	3378	6.58	1.79	10.10	70.02	1.88	9.63	1.54
	3380	6.52	2.14	9.11	66.35	1.70	14.18	2.27
	3382	7.12	1.35	9.32	68.86	1.27	12.08	1.93

Composition of hulls of American oats, arranged by States.

State.	Serial No.	Water.	Ash.	Undetermined.	Fiber.	Albuminoids.	Nitrogen.
		Per ct.	P. ct.	Per ct.	Per ct.	P. ct.	P. ct.
Maine	3133	4.60	4.30	65.89	28.36	1.75	.28
New Hampshire	3208	6.46	4.50	68.50	19.56	2.98	.48
	3209	3.90	4.36	70.48	19.16	2.10	.34
	3210	4.30	5.00	67.59	20.13	2.98	.48
Vermont	3322	4.08	5.40	68.99	18.20	3.33	.53
	3323	4.80	4.10	68.74	19.73	2.03	.42
	3324	3.60	3.60	73.50	17.46	1.75	.28
	3126	4.14	3.66	72.98	16.94	2.28	.36
Connecticut	3024	6.60	5.95	65.37	19.80	2.28	.36
	3028	5.60	4.44	67.13	20.20	2.03	.42
	3029	5.74	3.71	69.09	18.06	2.80	.45
Rhode Island	3294	5.00	4.50	73.12	15.10	2.28	.36
New York	3226	4.70	4.00	72.07	16.43	2.80	.45
	3231	4.50	4.90	68.52	18.93	3.15	.50
	3235	....	....	....	....	1.75	.28
	3243	5.00	4.40	74.02	13.95	2.60	.42
New Jersey	0214	2.90	6.30	68.46	19.19	3.15	.50
Pennsylvania	3282	3.68	4.30	70.54	18.85	2.63	.42
	3286	4.36	4.50	70.11	18.40	2.63	.42
	3286	4.30	3.20	69.10	21.15	1.75	.28
Ohio	3260	3.18	7.40	66.99	20.68	1.75	.28
	3261	3.52	5.60	70.54	16.84	3.50	.56
	3262	4.81	4.20	72.08	15.55	3.33	.53
	3267	5.58	5.80	69.57	17.12	1.93	.31
	3269	5.12	5.30	68.30	18.30	2.98	.48
	3270	4.84	7.70	66.80	18.56	2.10	.34
	3444	5.00	6.80	....	....	2.28	.30
Michigan	3153	4.96	3.84	68.55	20.02	2.63	.42
	3156	3.83	6.33	63.96	23.76	2.10	.34
	3158	4.82	5.20	69.55	18.50	1.93	.31
	3406	4.44	6.40	71.38	16.38	1.40	.22

Composition of hulls of American oats, arranged by States—Continued.

States.	Serial No.	Water.	Ash.	Undetermined.	Fiber.	Albuminoids.	Nitrogen.
		Per ct.	P. ct.	Per ct.	Per ct.	P. ct.	P. ct.
Indiana	3084	4.80	5.20	68.17	10.38	2.45	.39
Illinois	3055					2.10	.34
	3060	4.42	7.10	64.80	21.40	2.28	.36
	3062	7.70	5.70	67.31	14.56	4.73	.76
	3063	15.16	7.80	52.62	21.44	2.98	.48
	3067	5.16	7.20	67.44	17.02	2.28	.36
	3068	4.56	7.44	71.41	14.14	2.45	.39
	3068	5.12	5.88	65.78	21.12	2.10	.34
Wisconsin	3353	4.40	7.10	70.40	15.45	2.63	.42
	5357	4.70	6.90	69.11	17.71	1.58	.25
	3360	3.56	5.80	71.00	17.54	2.10	.34
	3361	2.20	6.50	70.35	19.20	1.75	.28
Minnesota	3166	4.71	7.10	64.41	21.85	1.93	.31
	3170	4.35	6.21	68.27	18.44	2.63	.42
	3172	5.30	5.40	68.75	18.04	2.45	.39
	3175	4.96	7.35			1.75	.28
	3176	6.54	7.00	67.70	16.76	2.10	.34
Iowa	3098	5.20	8.40			1.75	.28
	3104	4.50	6.22	64.70	22.14	2.45	.39
	3107	6.00	6.66	69.37	16.22	1.75	.28
Missouri	3191	5.13	6.55	69.11	16.58	2.63	.42
	3411	4.30	5.40	70.60	15.87	3.33	.53
Nebraska	3198	4.10	7.80	68.40	17.60	2.10	.34
Dakota	3035				18.12	1.75	.28
	3390	5.40	7.70	66.50	18.12	2.28	.36
Montana	3197	3.00	9.50	65.82	17.65	4.03	.64
	3415	4.40	4.48	70.25	19.12	1.75	.28
Maryland	3140	4.40	5.62	67.82	17.43	4.73	.76
	3141	4.00	4.02	64.68	24.42	2.28	.36
Delaware	3038				16.54	3.15	.50
Virginia	3334	3.08	3.90	74.41	16.16	2.45	.39
	3335	4.06	5.50	69.94	17.52	2.98	.48
	3337	5.10	3.70	64.97	23.42	2.81	.45
West Virginia	3345	4.30	5.60	67.38	20.62	2.10	.34
	3347	3.76	3.60	72.32	17.69	2.63	.42
North Carolina	3249	5.80	4.70	70.64	15.04	3.85	.62
	3251					2.80	.45
	3253	4.30	7.50	69.86	15.89	2.45	.39
	3255	5.40	6.50	72.13	12.82	3.15	.50
	3256	4.76	5.00	68.16	19.80	2.28	.36
	3257	4.82	5.90	71.63	15.37	2.28	.36
South Carolina	3295	3.86	3.90	76.04	13.50	2.10	.34
	3297	2.98	5.00	75.32	14.95	1.75	.28
	3299	4.10	5.40	73.62	13.90	2.98	.48
	3000	4.20	8.10	70.55	15.40	1.75	.28
	3402	6.00	5.80	71.21	11.91	5.08	.81
Kentucky	3116	5.10	4.80	64.80	23.55	1.75	.28
	3117	17.40	4.90	57.13	17.17	2.80	.45
	3122	9.90	5.30	60.68	19.22	4.90	.78
Tennessee	3304	8.90	6.50	67.30	14.85	2.45	.39
	3309	4.86	5.50	65.91	21.63	2.10	.34
Georgia	3047	5.71	5.31	68.47	18.06	2.45	.39
	3049	5.96	5.76	70.51	16.06	1.75	.28
	3049	5.70	5.15	71.24	15.46	2.45	.39
	3050	5.30	4.00	69.50	19.10	2.10	.34
	3052	5.50	4.40	67.17	20.48	2.45	.39
	3395	5.02	6.06	70.16	14.56	4.20	.67
Florida	3044	5.50	1.90	73.39	16.58	2.63	.42
	3045	5.78	2.98	74.79	14.70	1.75	.28
	3392	3.30	3.86	75.13	15.26	2.45	.39
Alabama	3092	14.94	4.80	63.17	14.75	2.28	.36
	3303	4.50	5.10	68.18	20.12	2.10	.34
Mississippi	3185	5.20	7.80	67.70	16.67	2.63	.42
	3187	5.40	6.75	68.20	17.72	1.93	.31
Louisiana	3126	15.60	4.60	58.13	19.57	2.10	.34
	3127	5.00	5.20	68.02	18.90	2.28	.36
Arkansas	3012	6.00	5.14	62.77	16.80	2.98	.48
Texas	3310	4.40	7.00	66.83	20.12	1.05	.17
	3311	4.20	6.20	72.62	14.35	2.63	.42
	3313	4.00	7.10	72.10	14.70	2.10	.34
	3315	3.90	7.70			2.63	.42
	3317	3.30	7.70	71.95	15.30	1.75	.28
	3430	4.40	7.50	71.56	15.31	1.23	.20
Colorado	3385	4.30	7.84	67.71	17.56	2.63	.42
	3583	4.04	5.40	65.92	22.54	2.10	.34
Utah	3321	4.70			20.59	3.50	.56
Washington Territory	3435	5.20	7.16	67.37	18.34	1.93	.31
Oregon	3277	5.12	4.80	71.37	16.96	1.75	.28
California	3374	4.20	6.02	71.63	16.40	1.75	.28

Average composition of American oats, arranged by States.

States.	Number of analyses.	Water.	Ash.	Oil.	Carbhy-drates.	Fiber.	Albumin-oids.	Nitrogen.
United States	179	6.93	2.15	8.14	67.00	1.38	14.31	2.28
Atlantic Slope	64	6.84	2.17	8.22	67.10	1.37	14.30	2.28
Northern States	92	7.07	2.19	8.02	66.88	1.37	14.47	2.32
Western States	54	6.98	2.19	7.91	67.06	1.37	14.49	2.32
Southern States	69	6.79	2.12	8.23	67.22	1.35	14.29	2.28
Northwestern States	8	7.38	2.23	8.54	66.96	1.28	13.61	2.18
Pacific Slope	18	6.71	2.10	8.87	67.78	1.53	13.01	2.08
Maine	3	7.19	1.91	8.55	66.40	1.77	14.18	2.27
New Hampshire	3	7.06	2.30	8.36	65.27	1.32	15.69	2.51
Vermont	4	6.33	2.00	8.06	66.15	1.34	15.62	2.50
Connecticut	4	6.54	2.30	8.06	68.07	1.47	13.56	2.17
Rhode Island	1	7.52	2.02	8.71	68.66	1.01	12.08	1.93
New York	9	7.46	2.14	8.02	66.53	1.44	14.41	2.31
New Jersey	2	7.42	2.29	7.14	66.55	1.29	15.31	2.45
Pennsylvania	4	7.10	2.36	8.00	65.85	1.32	15.37	2.46
Ohio	9	6.76	2.25	8.32	65.39	1.19	16.09	2.57
Michigan	6	7.11	2.35	7.74	67.61	1.19	14.00	2.24
Indiana	3	8.05	1.92	7.82	65.69	1.24	15.28	2.45
Illinois	9	6.19	2.34	7.64	67.69	1.55	14.59	2.34
Wisconsin	5	7.27	2.06	7.45	68.46	1.49	13.27	2.12
Minnesota	9	7.16	2.27	7.91	68.33	1.30	13.03	2.09
Iowa	7	7.01	2.03	8.02	66.72	1.44	14.78	2.37
Missouri	3	7.11	1.91	8.35	63.54	1.51	15.58	2.49
Nebraska	3	7.42	2.16	7.98	66.64	1.51	14.20	2.29
Dakota	5	6.74	2.25	8.16	67.39	1.28	14.28	2.27
Montana	3	8.44	2.20	9.18	66.23	1.29	12.66	2.03
Maryland	2	7.01	2.36	7.91	66.39	1.46	14.87	2.38
Delaware	1	5.94	2.27	7.75	66.09	1.35	16.60	2.66
Virginia	4	6.63	2.43	7.93	66.03	1.49	15.49	2.48
West Virginia	4	6.64	2.29	7.51	64.86	1.46	17.24	2.76
North Carolina	6	6.84	2.06	8.27	68.26	1.63	12.92	2.07
South Carolina	8	7.07	2.09	8.48	68.19	1.00	13.17	2.11
Kentucky	4	7.34	2.10	7.80	65.97	1.74	15.05	2.41
Tennessee	4	6.81	2.22	8.09	67.33	1.42	14.13	2.26
Georgia	8	6.15	2.28	8.54	67.65	1.35	14.13	2.26
Florida	5	6.03	2.08	8.49	67.85	1.37	14.18	2.27
Alabama	5	6.40	1.94	8.42	67.55	1.16	14.53	2.33
Mississippi	5	7.41	1.97	7.86	67.48	1.28	14.00	2.24
Louisiana	3	8.12	2.13	8.09	66.55	1.17	13.94	2.23
Arkansas	2	5.80	1.12	7.92	67.59	1.78	14.79	2.37
Texas	8	7.16	2.04	8.71	67.08	1.21	13.80	2.21
Colorado	4	6.06	2.31	7.80	67.50	1.10	15.23	2.44
Utah	2	6.67	2.39	8.49	68.30	1.72	12.43	1.99
Nevada	1	6.80	2.27	9.72	66.21	1.17	13.83	2.21
New Mexico	2	6.83	2.31	9.66	66.16	1.73	13.31	2.14
Washington Territory	2	6.82	1.67	9.28	69.96	1.51	10.76	1.72
Oregon	2	6.86	2.35	8.38	67.77	1.78	12.86	2.06
California	5	7.08	1.76	9.40	67.90	1.71	12.15	1.94

Average composition of hulls of oats, arranged by States.

State.	Number of analyses.	Water.	Ash.	Undeter-mined.	Fiber.	Albumin-oids.	Nitrogen.
United States	100	5.22	5.59	68.83	17.88	2.48	.40
Atlantic Slope	43	4.73	4.78	70.35	17.50	2.64	.42
Northern States	52	4.59	5.69	68.52	18.42	2.48	.40
Western States	33	4.99	6.39	67.68	18.30	2.44	.39
Southern States	43	5.71	5.40	69.20	17.15	2.54	.41
Northwestern States	17	4.57	6.25	68.80	18.35	2.03	.33
Pacific Slope	2	5.16	5.98	67.87	19.15	1.84	.30
Maine	1	4.00	4.30	65.99	23.36	1.75	.28
New Hampshire	3	4.88	4.62	68.19	19.62	2.69	.43
Vermont	4	4.15	4.19	71.08	18.08	2.50	.40
Connecticut	3	5.98	4.70	67.40	19.35	2.57	.41
Rhode Island	1	5.00	4.50	73.12	15.10	2.28	.36
New York	3	4.73	4.43	71.54	16.44	2.86	.40
New Jersey	1	2.90	6.30	68.46	19.19	3.15	.50
Pennsylvania	3	4.28	4.00	69.92	19.47	2.33	.37

Average composition of hulls of oats, arranged by States—Continued.

State.	Number of analyses.	Water.	Ash.	Undetermined.	Fiber.	Albuminoids.	Nitrogen.
Ohio	6	4.51	6.00	60.05	17.84	2.60	.42
Michigan	4	4.51	5.44	68.36	19.07	2.02	.32
Indiana	1	4.80	5.20	68.17	19.38	2.45	.30
Illinois	6	7.01	6.85	64.00	18.43	2.81	.45
Wisconsin	4	3.71	6.58	70.22	17.48	2.01	.32
Minnesota	4	5.24	6.43	67.28	18.77	2.28	.36
Iowa	2	5.25	6.43	67.04	19.18	2.10	.34
Nebraska	1	4.10	7.80	68.40	17.60	2.10	.34
Missouri	2	4.72	6.23	60.85	16.22	2.98	.48
Dakota	1	5.40	7.70	66.50	18.12	2.28	.36
Montana	2	7.40	6.99	68.04	18.38	2.89	.46
Maryland	2	4.20	5.12	66.24	20.94	3.50	.56
Virginia	3	4.08	4.67	60.77	19.03	2.75	.44
West Virginia	2	4.03	4.60	60.85	19.16	2.36	.38
North Carolina	5	5.02	5.92	70.48	15.78	2.80	.45
South Carolina	5	4.23	5.64	73.47	13.93	2.73	.44
Kentucky	3	10.80	5.00	60.87	20.18	3.15	.50
Tennessee	2	6.88	6.00	66.61	18.24	2.27	.36
Georgia	6	5.53	5.13	60.51	17.28	2.57	.41
Florida	3	4.86	2.10	74.44	15.51	2.28	.36
Alabama	2	9.72	4.98	65.68	17.43	2.19	.35
Mississippi	2	5.30	7.28	67.95	17.19	2.28	.36
Louisiana	2	10.30	4.90	63.38	10.23	2.19	.35
Arkansas	1	6.00	5.14	69.08	16.80	2.98	.48
Texas	5	4.06	7.22	71.01	15.96	1.75	.28
Colorado	2	4.17	6.02	66.82	20.03	2.36	.38
Washington Territory	1	5.20	7.16	67.37	18.34	1.93	.31
Oregon	1	5.12	4.80	68.37	19.96	1.75	.28
California	1	4.20	6.02	71.63	16.40	1.75	.28

The chemical composition of the specimens appears from the preceding data to be rather surprising. It was reasonable to suppose that as oats deteriorate so readily, and are apparantly so easily influenced by their environment, great variations would be found in their composition under different climatic conditions, as is the case with wheats. Brewer remarks in his census report that a hundred or more analyses would be requisite to set at rest all questions in regard to this grain, and that they would be an extremely valuable contribution to our knowledge of the comparative nutritive values of the oats grown in different portions of the United States and their relative economic values. One hundred and seventy-nine analyses have been made, and we learn that there is not that variation in the oat kernel itself which was expected to be due to climatic condition. The proportion of husk to kernel and the compactness of the grain prove to be the all-important factors, and the weight per bushel the best means of judging of the value of the grain.

The only peculiarities noticed are that the eighteen specimens from the Pacific slope are lower in albuminoids and richer in fiber than the averages for other parts of the country. The average for the hulls from the West show the presence of more ash than in those from the East, and more fiber, and, like the kernels, they are slightly deficient in albuminoids. Actual analysis of the mixed remainder from the individual analyses of the hulls furnished the following results:

	North.	South.	West.
	Per ct.	Per ct.	Per ct.
Water	7.71	7.83	8.10
Ash	5.57	5.50	0.22
Oil	.79	.74	1.01
Undetermined	62.47	63.84	60.09
Crude fiber	20.83	19.64	21.45
Albuminoids	2.63	2.45	3.13
	100.00	100.00	100.00

The small number from the West contained rather more albuminoids than the average results for that part of the country, but for the other sections there is a close agreement. In these samples, oil was determined and found to be extremely small in amount, following the percentage of albuminoids, the largest amount of both of these constituents being in the Western hulls, and there seems to be a more or less intimate connection between them.

Of all the cereals this is the richest in oil and albuminoids, the average for the former being 8.14 per cent. and for the latter 14.31; of course diminished relatively in the grain as fed, the average composition of which would probably be, as calculated from the average for each portion—

	Kernel.	Hull.	Whole grain.
	Per cent.	Per cent.	Per cent.
Water	4.85	1.57	6.42
Ash	1.50	1.68	3.18
Oil	5.70	.24	5.94
Carbhydrates	46.96	20.41	67.37
Crude fiber	.97	5.36	6.33
Albuminoids	10.02	.74	10.76
	70.00	30.00	100.00

An average of 20 analyses of oats in the husk given by Brewer and 153 given by Koenig are given as follows for comparison:

	Brewer.	Koenig.	Richardson.
	Per cent.	Per cent.	Per cent.
Water	10.56	12.37	6.42
Ash	2.95	3.02	3.18
Oil	4.97	5.23	6.04
Carbhydrates	61.10	57.78	66.67
Crude fiber	9.01	11.19	6.33
Albuminoids	11.41	10.41	10.76

The average albuminoids in the grains as fed, calculated in this same manner, is as follows for different sections:

	Per cent.
Northern States	10.96
Southern States	10.66
Pacific slope	9.60
Atlantic slope	10.76
Western States	11.24

The lowness of the Pacific slope is purely climatic, as has been found to be the case with all the cereals. In appearance the oats from that section are the finest. The fullness of the husk in the Western States or the plumpness of the grain make this the richest in albuminoids as it is fed. The South is poorest for reasons which have been mentioned. That these figures are entirely dependent on the percentage of husk, and not on peculiarities of the kernel, a study of their analyses will show; for, among 179, only 3 fell below 10 per cent. of albuminoids, 4 below 11 per cent., and 12 below 12 per cent., while at the same time only 13 are above 17 per cent., and 23 above 16 per cent.; that is to say, all but 28, or 84.4 per cent., are within the limits of 12 and 16 per cent., a small variation, although the albuminoids are higher in amount than wheat; and as the averages for the different States and sections of the country do not vary far from 14.3 per cent., with the exception of the Pacific coast, oats cannot be said, as far as the grain itself is concerned, to be in chemical composition very susceptible to their environment, although extremes widely apart are found. These were as follows:

Extremes in composition of kernels of oats.

	Highest.	State.	Lowest.	State.
	Per cent.		Per cent.	
Water	11.13	Montana	4.07	Arkansas.
Ash	2.94	Michigan	.87	Iowa.
Oil	11.20	Texas	6.50	Virginia.
Carbohydrates	71.91	North Carolina	62.82	Texas and Missouri.
Crude fiber	2.08	Kentucky and Oregon	.88	South Carolina.
Albuminoids	19.44	Ohio	9.10	North Carolina.

The highest percentage of albuminoids was 1.41 per cent. higher than has been found in any other cereal in this country, and the lowest 2 per cent. higher than was found in wheat.

The analysis of the heaviest and largest, of those having the greatest and least weight per bushel, of those having highest and lowest percentage of albuminoids and of the smallest in size and in weight per bushel, have been selected as a study of the effect of these contrasts on the chemical composition.

Composition of specimens exhibiting extreme characteristics.

	Serial number.	State.	Weight of 100 kernels.	Husk.	Weight per bushel.	Water.	Ash.	Oil.	Crude fiber.	Albuminoids.
			Gr'ms	P. ct.	Lbs.	P. ct.	P. ct.	P. ct.	P. ct.	P. ct.	P. ct.
Smallest	3200	Nebr	1.512	31.21	29.7	7.32	2.24	8.72	66.39	1.33	14.00
Largest	3277	Oreg	3.786	40.85	43.3	7.01	2.42	7.87	66.80	2.07	13.83
Cleanest	3041	Fla	2.880	32.87	31.5	5.83	2.52	7.68	68.93	1.56	13.48
Chaffiest	3185	Miss	2.113	25.40	38.2	7.05	2.10	7.81	67.32	1.54	14.18
Highest per cent. of kernel	3435	Wash	3.148	20.72	43.2	6.55	1.55	10.57	68.36	1.07	11.90
Lowest per cent. of kernel	3391	Dak	2.372	44.63	38.8	8.75	2.15	9.47	66.17	1.56	11.90
Highest albuminoids	3262	Ohio	2.670	39.17	40.0	6.78	2.07	7.40	63.21	1.10	19.44
Lowest albuminoids	3249	N.C	2.060	29.50	47.8	7.78	2.02	7.32	71.91	1.87	9.10
Heaviest weight per bushel	3020	Col	2.958	30.24	48.8	4.80	2.08	7.27	66.82	1.00	18.03
Lightest weight per bushel	3002	Ala	3.068	31.66	24.7	6.59	1.80	8.98	66.20	1.20	15.23
Average weight for United States.		U.S	2.507	30.03	37.2	6.93	2.15	8.14	67.09	1.38	14.31

From the preceding figures nothing can be deduced which shows any such difference as we might expect between the largest and smallest oats. between the cleanest and most chaffy, or between those having the highest and lowest proportion of kernel in the grain. The weight per bushel of the specimen having the lowest percentage of albuminoids is extraordinarily high, while that containing the highest percentage is also above the average. Differences, too, between the weights per bushel of the extreme specimens are in no wise connected with their chemical composition. The largest and one of the finest and heaviest oats from Oregon had nearly the maximum of husk, and, while the lowest proportion of husk corresponded, of course, with a high weight per bushel, the largest proportion of husks was coincident with a weight per bushel above the average.

An immense number of conditions seem, therefore, to affect the characteristics of this grain, and while in many ways, at first glance, it seems to be less changeable than one would expect, on examination it seems to be quite largely influenced by all the circumstances of its environment, and in a more irregular way than wheat.

Throughout all the averages it will be seen that oats are much drier than other grains, owing largely to their small size. In ash and fiber they are not exceptionable.

Grown in the same locality, under similar conditions, two specimens of different varieties may vary considerably as was found to be the case with wheat. For examples the following determinations of albuminoids will serve:

State.	Serial No.	Albuminoids.
		Per cent.
Pennsylvania	3286_1	13.65
Pennsylvania	3286_2	15.75
Georgia	3049_1	13.48
Georgia	3049_2	14.88
Georgia	3049_3	15.93
Georgia	3049_4	14.18
Illinois	3068_1	14.35
Illinois	3068_2	15.05
Minnesota	3175_1	13.83
Minnesota	3175_2	13.48

In the last locality there is little difference; but there is no reason why in some cases, in fact many, there should not be an agreement where the varieties possess similar capabilities of assimilation.

One specimen, Serial No. 3200, from Nebraska, was by accident analyzed twice from the same bag. The results show the differences which may be expected in work of this kind which we have had in hand:

		No. 1.	No. 2.
Weight of 100 kernels	grams	1.582	1.512
Clean grain	per cent	97.20	97.40
Kernels	do	68.30	68.79
Hulls	do	31.70	31.21
Weight, per bushel	pounds	30.2	29.7
Water	per cent	6.90	7.32
Ash	do	2.21	2.24
Oil	do	8.32	8.72
Carbhydrates	do	66.72	66.39
Crude fiber	do	1.85	1.33
Albuminoids	do	14.00	14.00

It may be said that the duplication was unknown to any one until after tabulation, and the coincidence in all the results, which are not variable in the preparation of the sample for analysis, was even better than is to be expected. Moisture, even in the tightest-stoppered bottles, is liable to change, as has been shown in previous reports, and with fiber, when present in so small amount, it is difficult to secure duplicates which will not at times differ as much as half of one per cent. Ash, oil, and albuminoids admit of determination with almost the accuracy of inorganic work.

A study of the analysis having shown that variations in chemical composition for any one season are not accompanied by any corresponding change in physical qualities, that the variations in any one locality are often quite as large as over the whole country, and that the Pacific coast alone produces a grain whose average composition is to any degree different from that of other States, it seems probable that the differences in composition are as largely due to soil as to other causes.

In this connection reference must be made to the recent valuable and instructive experiments with oats, conducted at the experiment at Halle, Germany, by Dr. Maercker, the results of which have appeared in the Zeitschrift des landwirthschaftlichen Verein der Provinz Sachsen, from which it has been learned that the condition of the soil and manures have a marked effect not only on the yield, but the composition of the crop.

The following are some of the valuable conclusions reached in 1883:

(1) 38 pounds of oats sown to the acre, in spite of a heavy application of artificial manure, was not able to give so high a product as the same area sown with 84 pounds.

(2) The application of phosphoric acid alone did not increase the product essentially, in spite of the fact that the experimental field was in good condition and did not suffer at all from the lack of nitrogen.

(3) The application of nitrogenous manure in general increased the product decidedly, proportional to the amount of applied nitrogen.

(4) Small or large quantities of phosphoric acid, together with weak nitrogenous manuring, furnished in the form of Chili saltpeter, showed themselves of paying efficacy.

(5) With strong nitrogenous manuring neither large nor small applications of phosphoric acid brought about any action worth mentioning.

(6) The product of grain and straw was increased in about equal degrees by the artificial manuring.

(7) The proportion of corn to straw was by thick sowing, on the average 47 to 53 or 1 to 1.13; by thin sowing, 45 to 55 or 1 to 1.22.

(8) The harvest showed throughout a tolerably low percentage of nitrogen, in the case of the straw; not, however, an extremely low one, plainly because the rooting up of the weeds and the strengthening of the stems of the oat plant by drilling and harrowing produced plants which were, on the average, poor in nitrogen.

(9) By thin sowing the plants were somewhat richer in nitrogen than by thick.

(10) The application of phosphoric acid alone was not able to raise the percentage of nitrogen.

(11) On the contrary, the percentage of nitrogen was essentially raised by the application of nitrogenous manures.

(12) An application of phosphate manures, together with that of nitrogenous manures, did not alter the percentage of nitrogen.

(13) The greater the harvest the greater also was the percentage of nitrogen in the grain and the straw; from this it appears that the more that was harvested, the better was the quality of the product. A rational method of manuring brings about, not alone greater crops, but also better grain.

(14) The small and poorly-shaped grain harvested with the application of large amounts of nitrogen, and in consequence of this somewhat stalled, possess a higher percentage of nitrogen than the fully-developed grain; they cannot, therefore, be looked upon as of less value.

(15) By an application of phosphate manure alone the percentage of oil in the grain was not increased.

(16) On the contrary, by an application of nitrogenous manure alone the oil was decreased.

(17) A weak application of phosphoric acid at the same time with one of nitrogen reproduced the original amount of oil; a stronger application of phosphate even increased it, plainly through assistance in ripening.

(18) The grain manured more strongly with nitrogen was on the whole somewhat richer in fiber and somewhat poorer in nitrogen free nutrients than the grain manured less with nitrogen and more with phosphoric acid.

(19) By a rational method of manuring the albuminoid content of the crop can be almost doubled.

(20) In these experiments 55 per cent. of the nitrogen applied in the manures was recovered in the crop.

In his report on the work of the experiment station in 1884, Dr. Maercker continues, in regard to the investigations:

During this year the same experiments have been carried out (with oats) again. It is the second year of which I here give an account, and the results of the first year are completely confirmed:

(1) That plants relatively poor in nitrogen have been obtained by drilling and harrowing.

(2) That thin sowing has in no case produced as much as thicker sowing.

(3) That a nitrogenous manuring raises strongly the percentage of nitrogen in oats. Further that in this year it has been found that, by manuring with phosphoric acid, the albuminoids were materially decreased, although the formation of starch has been

increased. Phosphoric acid hastens the ripening and in general the tendency of the plants to fill out the kernels completely, on which account there is more starch and less protein. Plants relatively poor in nitrogen are therefore produced.

The availability of plant-food is therefore the prime cause of there being so many variations in any one locality corresponding to the soil and manuring on which the crops are dependent.

Our analyses of oats extend over only one year, but Dr. Maercker in two has shown, as our work has with wheat, that "oats appear to be extraordinarily dependent, even in the same locality, in their composition, on the climatic conditions ruling during the opening period." The crops raised in 1882 and 1883, in exactly the same manner, compared in albuminoids, are as follows:

	Per cent.
Unmanured, 1882	7.8
Unmanured, 1883	10.2
600 pounds per acre of Chili saltpeter, 1882	10.5
600 pounds per acre of Chili saltpeter, 1883	12.8

The difference between these figures for the same year illustrates the effect of nitrogenous fertilizers on the percentage of that element in the grain, it being greater in the manured grain by 2.7 per cent. in 1882 and 2.6 per cent. in 1883; and at the same time the effect of the variation in the seasons is as markedly visible.

Comparing the production per acre with the percentage of nitrogen on the grain it was found that those varieties giving the largest yield were poorest in nitrogen, and the reverse.

No.	Name.	Pounds per acre.	Albuminoids.
			Per cent.
1	Anderbecker	3,737	8.7
2	Danish	3,591	8.5
3	Original Probsteier	3,564	9.3
4	Lüneburger clay	3,496	9.8
5	Hallet's Canadian	3,393	11.7
6	Australian	3,005	11.2
7	Hopetown	3,044	12.2
8	Black Californian	2,928	9.8
9	White Tartarian Swedish	2,874	10.1
10	Kylberg pedigree	2,839	9.5

These results, calculated to the amount of nitrogen harvested per acre by the whole plant, explain the differences by showing that all varieties collect about the same amount; consequently, if there is much grain the nitrogen is divided up among it, or if there is much straw the grain is thereby deprived of a certain amount. In 1883 the results were quite different from this. High yields had high percentages of nitrogen, as appears from conclusion 13, previously given. This point, therefore, hardly seems to be entirely settled, but to be largely dependent on the climatic conditions of varying seasons.

For more complete details, reference must be made to the original report upon the experiments, which are models of what should be undertaken in our own country. It is of interest, however, to copy certain tables which are of value for comparison with our own analyses and for filling out our knowledge of the plant in directions towards which our investigations did not extend.

EFFECT OF THICK AND THIN SOWING.

The following tables give the chemical composition of the grain harvested after thick and thin sowing. The average weight per bushel in both cases was 36.7 lbs. All the analyses are calculated to 15 per cent. of water, and the units of nutritive value, being calculated on a German basis, are to us of only relative value.

Composition of crops.
GRAIN.
[Thick sowing, 44 kilograms per hectare.]

Manuring.	No.	Ash.	Oil.	Carbhydrates.	Crude fiber.	Albuminoids.	Units of nutritive value.
Unmanured	1	3.1	3.8	60.0	10.4	7.7	118.0
— kilograms Chili saltpeter, 200 kilograms superphosphate..	2	3.7	3.9	58.7	10.0	8.7	121.7
— kilograms Chili saltpeter, 400 kilograms superphosphate..	3	3.2	3.9	59.4	10.5	8.0	110.9
200 kilograms Chili saltpeter, — kilograms superphosphate..	4	3.3	3.1	58.7	10.6	9.3	120.7
300 kilograms Chili saltpeter, — kilograms superphosphate..	5	3.1	3.0	59.2	9.8	9.9	124.2
400 kilograms Chili saltpeter, — kilograms superphosphate..	6	3.0	2.9	58.2	10.4	10.5	125.2
200 kilograms Chili saltpeter, 200 kilograms superphosphate..	7	3.1	3.5	59.7	9.4	9.3	123.7
300 kilograms Chili saltpeter, 200 kilograms superphosphate..	8	3.2	3.4	58.6	10.2	9.6	123.6
400 kilograms Chili saltpeter, 200 kilograms superphosphate..	9	3.1	3.5	56.9	11.1	10.4	126.4
200 kilograms Chili saltpeter, 400 kilograms superphosphate..	10	3.0	4.3	58.9	8.6	10.2	131.4
300 kilograms Chili saltpeter, 400 kilograms superphosphate..	11	3.0	4.3	58.2	9.3	10.2	130.7
400 kilograms Chili saltpeter, 400 kilograms superphosphate..	12	3.5	4.2	56.4	11.0	9.8	126.4

[Thin sowing, 76 kilograms per hectare.]

Manuring.	No.	Ash.	Oil.	Carbhydrates.	Crude fiber.	Albuminoids.	Units of nutritive value.
Unmanured	13	3.3	3.8	59.6	10.4	7.9	118.1
— kilograms Chili saltpeter, 400 kilograms superphosphate..	14	3.1	4.0	60.0	10.4	7.5	117.5
400 kilograms Chili saltpeter, — kilograms superphosphate..	15	3.3	3.1	58.8	9.9	9.9	123.8
200 kilograms Chili saltpeter, 200 kilograms superphosphate..	16	3.1	3.7	59.7	9.2	9.3	124.7
400 kilograms Chili saltpeter, 200 kilograms superphosphate..	17	3.1	3.7	58.0	9.9	10.3	128.0
400 kilograms Chili saltpeter, 400 kilograms superphosphate..	18	3.1	3.6	59.3	9.6	9.4	124.3

CHAFF.
[Thick sowing, 44 kilograms per hectare.]

Manuring.	No.	Ash.	Oil.	Carbhydrates.	Crude fiber.	Albuminoids.	Units of nutritive value.
Unmanured	1	13.9	.....	41.9	24.9	4.3	63.4
— kilograms Chili saltpeter, 200 kilograms superphosphate.	2	14.1	.....	41.7	24.4	4.8	65.7
— kilograms Chili saltpeter, 400 kilograms superphosphate.	3	14.0	.....	41.8	24.9	4.3	63.3
200 kilograms Chili saltpeter, — kilograms superphosphate.	4	14.3	.....	42.2	23.7	4.8	66.2
300 kilograms Chili saltpeter, — kilograms superphosphate.	5	13.6	.....	41.3	24.9	5.2	67.3
400 kilograms Chili saltpeter, — kilograms superphosphate.	6	15.0	.....	40.7	24.0	5.3	67.2
200 kilograms Chili saltpeter, 200 kilograms superphosphate.	7	13.0	.....	42.8	23.9	5.3	60.3
300 kilograms Chili saltpeter, 200 kilograms superphosphate.	8	13.7	.....	41.8	24.1	5.4	68.8
400 kilograms Chili saltpeter, 200 kilograms superphosphate.	9	15.1	.....	40.4	23.6	5.9	69.9
200 kilograms Chili saltpeter, 400 kilograms superphosphate.	10	14.6	.....	41.8	23.6	5.0	66.8
300 kilograms Chili saltpeter, 400 kilograms superphosphate.	11	14.2	.....	41.9	23.9	5.0	66.9
400 kilograms Chili saltpeter, 400 kilograms superphosphate.	12	13.9	.....	42.3	23.1	5.7	70.8

[Thin sowing, 76 kilograms per hectare.]

Manuring.	No.	Ash.	Oil.	Carbhydrates.	Crude fiber.	Albuminoids.	Units of nutritive value.
Unmanured	13	13.8	.....	43.2	23.5	4.5	65.7
— kilograms Chili saltpeter, 400 kilograms superphosphate.	14	14.1	.....	42.1	23.9	4.9	66.6
400 kilograms Chili saltpeter, — kilograms superphosphate.	15	13.9	.....	41.6	24.2	5.3	68.8
200 kilograms Chili saltpeter, 200 kilograms superphosphate.	16	13.1	.....	43.8	23.5	4.6	65.8
400 kilograms Chili saltpeter, 200 kilograms superphosphate.	17	14.2	.....	42.4	24.0	4.4	64.4
400 kilograms Chili saltpeter, 400 kilograms superphosphate.	18	14.4	.....	41.4	24.8	4.4	63.4

[Kilo. per hectare + .8923 = lbs per acre.]

Composition of crops—Continued.

STRAW.

[Thick sowing, 44 kilograms per hectare.]

Manured.	No.	Ash.	Oil.	Carbyhdrates.	Crude fiber.	Albuminoids.	Units of nutritive value.
Unmanured	1	5.7	....	38.6	38.9	1.83	48.1
— kilograms Chili saltpeter, 200 kilograms superphosphate	2	5.9	....	36.9	40.5	1.66	45.4
— kilograms Chili saltpeter, 400 kilograms superphosphate	3	5.8	....	39.2	39.5	1.51	46.7
200 kilograms Chili saltpeter, — kilograms superphosphate	4	5.9	....	39.3	38.2	1.55	47.3
300 kilograms Chili saltpeter, — kilograms superphosphate	5	6.2	....	37.7	39.5	1.62	45.7
400 kilograms Chili saltpeter, —0 kilograms superphosphate	6	6.2	....	33.7	43.2	1.86	43.2
200 kilograms Chili saltpeter, 200 kilograms superphosphate	7	5.8	....	37.9	39.7	1.62	45.9
300 kilograms Chili saltpeter, 200 kilograms superphosphate	8	6.4	....	37.1	39.8	1.71	45.6
400 kilograms Chili saltpeter, 200 kilograms superphosphate	9	6.1	....	37.4	39.5	2.04	47.4
200 kilograms Chili saltpeter, 400 kilograms superphosphate	10	5.9	....	36.4	41.2	1.51	43.9
300 kilograms Chili saltpeter, 400 kilograms superphosphate	11	5.7	....	36.0	41.9	1.36	43.0
400 kilograms Chili saltpeter, 400 kilograms superphosphate	12	5.9	....	38.4	39.2	1.69	46.9

[Thin sowing, 76 kilograms per hectare.]

Manured.	No.	Ash.	Oil.	Carbyhdrates.	Crude fiber.	Albuminoids.	Units of nutritive value.
Unmanured	13	5.5	....	38.1	40.1	1.27	44.6
— kilograms Chili saltpeter, 400 kilograms superphosphate	14	5.3	....	39.0	39.5	1.24	45.2
400 kilograms Chili saltpeter, — kilograms superphosphate	15	5.4	....	37.7	40.4	1.49	45.2
200 kilograms Chili saltpeter, 200 kilograms superphosphate	16	5.2	....	38.2	40.3	1.27	44.7
400 kilograms Chili saltpeter, 200 kilograms superphosphate	17	5.5	....	39.0	38.9	1.63	47.0
400 kilograms Chili saltpeter, 400 kilograms superphosphate	18	5.6	....	37.9	40.0	1.46	45.4

COMPOSITION OF THE GRAIN.

	Thin sowing.			Thick sowing.			By Julius Kühn.		
	Maximum.	Minimum.	Mean.	Maximum.	Minimum.	Mean.	Maximum.	Minimum.	Mean.
Ash	3.7	3.0	3.2	3.3	3.1	3.2	2.7	2.7	2.7
Oil	4.3	2.9	3.7	4.0	3.1	3.7	9.2	4.4	6.0
Carbyhdrates	60.0	56.4	58.6	60.0	58.0	59.3	72.7	48.0	56.6
Crude fiber	11.1	8.6	10.1	10.4	9.2	9.9	16.1	4.1	9.0
Albuminoids	10.5	7.7	9.5	10.3	7.5	9.0	18.5	6.3	12.0

COMPOSITION OF THE CHAFF.

	Thin sowing.			Thick sowing.			By Julius Kühn.		
	Maximum.	Minimum.	Mean.	Maximum.	Minimum.	Mean.	Maximum.	Minimum.	Mean.
Ash	15.1	13.0	14.1	13.1	13.1	13.9	11.0	11.0	11.0
Oil	....	....	....	....	....	....	....	....	....
Carbyhdrates	42.8	40.4	41.7	43.8	41.4	42.5	43.2	28.2	37.4
Crude fiber	24.9	23.1	24.1	24.8	23.5	24.0	35.1	25.9	31.7
Albuminoids	5.9	4.3	5.1	5.3	4.4	4.6	7.0	3.7	4.9

COMPOSITION OF THE STRAW.

	Thin sowing.			Thick sowing.			By Julius Kühn.		
	Maximum.	Minimum.	Mean.	Maximum.	Minimum.	Mean.	Maximum.	Minimum.	Mean.
Ash	6.2	5.7	6.0	5.6	5.2	5.4	4.4	4.4	4.4
Carbyhdrates	39.2	33.7	37.3	39.0	37.9	38.3	48.9	24.9	35.6
Crude fiber	43.2	38.9	40.1	40.4	38.9	39.9	50.2	30.0	39.7
Albuminoids	2.0	1.4	1.7	1.6	1.2	1.4	7.0	1.3	4.0

All these results show how variable the oat plant is both for the same year and for different seasons, and that conclusions drawn from the studies of specimens of one season's growth alone may be quite reversed by a wider examination.

Many causes, however, influencing the variations in quality have been explained and the field for future investigation made evident.

RYE.

Of this cereal, which is of the least importance of any grown in the United States, only 5 samples have been analyzed up to the present time. To supply this deficiency, 56 specimens were collected from the Department correspondents and the principal rye-producing States, at the same time with those of oats and barley.

Their sources were as follows:

53

Sources of rye.

State.	No.	Name.	Sown.	Harvested.	County.	Town.	Sender.	Remarks.
Colorado	5021	Unknown	Sept. 1 to Oct. 20	July 10 to 20	Custer	Wetmore	J. W. Coleman	
Connecticut	5024	Common	Sept. to Oct	July 1 to 10	New Haven	South Britain	W. L. Mitchell	
	5027	...do	Sept. 20	July 20	New London	Groton	J. J. Cupp	
	5028	Common White	...do	July 22	Litchfield	West Cornwall	T. S. Gold	
	5029	Winter	Sept. 1 to Oct. 15	July 5 to 20	Fairfield	Green's Farms	W. J. Jennings	
Georgia	5052	Georgia	Sept. 1 to Dec. 1	May 15	Brooks	Quitman	J. G. McCall	
Illinois	5060	(?)	End of Sept.	July	Will	Creto	J. O. Piepenbrink	Seed from Department.
	5062	White	Sept. 10 to Oct. 20	July 20 to 25	Jo Daviess	Howardsville	A. M. Durkee	
	5063	Common Winter	Sept. 1 to 15	July 1 to 15	Ogle	Baileyville	W. B. Derrick	
	5066	Common	Sept. 10	July 4	Livingstone	Cayuga	E. W. Pearson	
	5067	White Winter	Sept. 15 to Oct. 20	July 1	Lee	Dixon	Abram Brown	
	5068	Common Black	Oct. 1	...do	La Salle	Tonica	L. A. Burgess	
	5070	Winter	Sept. 1 to 25	July 5	Kankakee	Momence	A. L. Miner	
	5075	...do	Nov. 1	June 10	Du Page	Downer's Grove	H. L. Bush	
	5079	Common White	Sept	July 25	Bureau	Princeton	D. Knight	
Indiana	5086	Spring	Apr. 10	June 25 to July 1	Elkhart	Gosheu	P. F. Nye	
Iowa	5094	Common	Sept. 20 to Oct. 10	July 1 to 15	Taylor	Conway	J. L. Herr	
	5097	Summer Hill	Sept. 20 to 30	July 10	Sac	Wall Lake	J. H. Hoebing	
	5107	White Winter	Mid. Sept. to mid. Oct.		Clinton	Bryant	Dan. Conrad	
Kentucky	5445	White	Oct. 1 to 31	June 15 to 30	Lyon	Larchwood	Larchwood estate	
	5116	Black	...do	...do	Lawrence	Louise	J. M. Clayton	
Maryland	5140	(?)	Oct. 1 to 10	July 15 to 20	Frederick	Frederick	H. C. Brown	
	5141	Early White	Sept. to Oct	July 1	Garrett	Oakland	P. Hamill	
Minnesota	5163		Oct. 6	July 27	Todd	Long Prairie	L. S. Hoadley	
	5168	Canada White	Aug. 28	Aug. 4	Anoka	Anoka	A. Small	
	5170	(?)	(?)	(?)	Fillmore	Fillmore	G. W. Knight	
Missouri	5188	White	Sept. to Oct	June 15 to 25	Atchison	Langdon	R. Buckhein	
Nebraska	5198	Common, mixed	Sept	July 1	Antelope	Neligh	F. H. Trowbridge	
New Jersey	5214	Common White	Sept	June 20 to 25	Somerset	Blawenburg	D. C. Vorhees	
	5215	Jersey	Sept 15 to Oct. 15	July 4 to 15	Morris	Morristown	J. R. Runyan	
	5223	Winter	Sept. 10 to 10	July 6	Rensselaer	(†)	W. P. Rowe	
New York	5225	...do	Sept. 10	July 10	Albany	Slingerland's	C. L. G. Blessing	
	5231	Native	Sep. 1 to 20	July 15 to Aug. 1	Dutchess	Mount Ross	Benjamin Wilbur	
	5234	White	Aug. 20 to Sept. 10	First of July	Saratoga	Greenfield Centre	B. S. Robinson	
	5235	Common	Sept	July 1	Schoharie	Schoharie	I. C. Van Tuyl	
North Carolina	5246	White	Sept. to Oct	June to July	Henderson	Hendersonville	Joseph Livingstone	
Ohio	5250	...do	Sept	July 1	Ashe	Beaver Creek	J. F. Taylor	
	5260	Common	Sept. 1 to 20	June 1 to 15	Butler	Gano	Joseph Allen	
	5269	Black Fall	Oct. 18	July 1	Wood	Mermill	Andrew Welton	
Pennsylvania	5282	White	Sept. to Oct	July 1	Union	Lewisburg	J. A. Gundy	Raised for straw.
	5286	Common	Sept. 18 to Oct	July 10	Butler	Butler	H. I. Berg	
Rhode Island	5286½	Canada						From Department in 1882.
	5290	Winter	Oct. 1	July	Washington	Wickford	B. H. Lawton	
South Carolina	5299	Common	Aug	May	Laurens	Goodgion's Fact'y	J. S. Wolff	

54

Sources of rye—Continued.

State.	No.	Name.	Sown.	Harvested.	County.	Town.	Sender.	Remarks.
Vermont	5322	Common New England	Sept. 4		Bennington	Manchester	G. G. Burton	
	5323	White winter	Sept. 18 to Nov	July 20 to Aug 20	Windsor	Pomfret	Crosby Miller	
	5324	Winter	Last of Sept to Oct. 15.	Last June to July	Washington	Montpelier	A. D. Arens	
Virginia	5334	do	Oct.		Floyd	Floyd Court-House	Benjamin Phleger	
Washington	5341	Department	Aug. 15 to Nov. 1	July 20	Skagit	Lyman	L. Everett	
West Virginia	5346	Pennsylvania White	Oct. 15 to 20	June 25 to July 10	Ohio	Rony's Point	T. J. Orr	Poor on account of drought.
	5348	White	Apr. 1	July 1 to 4	Greenbrier	Lewisburg	H. Handly	
Wisconsin	5351	Common		Aug. 1	Chippewa	Eagle Point	John Bates	
	5353	(?)						
	5357	Black Winter	Sept. 10	July 12	Lafayette	Fayette	S. E. Roberts	
	5360	White	Oct. 1	(?)	Fond du Lac	Metomen	E. Reynolds	
	5361			(?)	Dodge	Burnett	H. Sawyer	Little grown here.

55

The specimens previously described have been examined physically and chemically with the following results:

Weight of 100 grains and per bushel of American ryes.

State.	Serial number.	Weight of 100 grains.	Weight per bushel.	State.	Serial number.	Weight of 100 grains.	Weight per bushel.
Vermont	5322	2.100	62.3	Illinois	5070	1.640	58.1
	5323	2.400	64.1		5075	1.840	59.4
	5324	2.100	58.0		5079	1.670	60.1
Connecticut	5024	2.410		Wisconsin	5351	2.000	60.4
	5027	1.990	60.2		5353	2.100	62.6
	5028	2.380	61.5		5357	1.690	60.6
	5029	2.520	62.8		5360	1.850	60.2
Rhode Island	5290	2.150			5361	2.700	61.9
New York	5223	2.240	60.4	Minnesota	5167	2.130	60.8
	5225	2.320	56.2		5168	2.780	62.2
	5231	2.310	60.1		5179	1.900	
	5234	2.160	62.6	Iowa	5094	1.590	60.2
	5235	2.060	63.1		5097	1.300	58.2
New Jersey	5214	1.700	63.3		5107	2.100	60.2
	5215	2.600	59.1	Nebraska	5198	1.300	60.3
Pennsylvania	5282	2.420	59.3	Maryland	5140	2.170	62.0
	5286	2.810	62.3		5141	2.570	59.9
	5286²	2.590	63.5	Virginia	5334	1.920	60.2
Ohio	5260	2.179	61.6	West Virginia	5346	2.430	62.8
	5260	2.080	61.7		5348	2.060	59.4
Indiana	5086	2.100	63.5	North Carolina	5248	1.870	62.1
Illinois	5060	1.910	60.4		5250	1.670	62.3
	5062	1.870	60.7	South Carolina	5299	2.040	
	5063	1.720	61.7	Kentucky	5116	1.580	
	5066	1.410	57.8		5116²	2.250	
	5067	2.100	60.0	Colorado	5021	1.810	61.4
	5068	1.820	58.7	Georgia	5052	1.240	
				Washington Ter	5341	3.450	

Average weight per bushel and of 100 grains of American ryes.

State.	Number of determinations.	Weight of 100 grains.	Weight per bushel.	State.	Number of determinations.	Weight of 100 grains.	Weight per bushel.
United States	56	2.074	60.9	Wisconsin	5	2.070	61.1
Atlantic Slope	25	2.189	61.2	Minnesota	3	2.270	61.5
Northern States	43	2.074	60.8	Iowa	3	1.660	59.5
Southern States	11	1.981	61.2	Missouri	1		62.6
Western States	25	1.745	60.0	Nebraska	1	1.300	60.3
Pacific Slope	2	2.030	61.4	Maryland	2	2.370	61.0
Vermont	3	2.200	61.7	Virginia	1	1.920	60.1
Connecticut	4	2.320	61.5	West Virginia	2	2.250	61.1
Rhode Island	1	2.150		North Carolina	2	1.770	62.2
New York	5	2.220	60.5	South Carolina	1	2.040	
New Jersey	2	2.150	61.2	Kentucky	2	1.920	
Pennsylvania	3	2.610	61.7	Georgia	1	1.240	
Ohio	2	2.130	61.7	Colorado	1	1.810	61.4
Indiana	1	2.100	63.5	Washington Ter	1	3.450	
Illinois	9	1.780	59.7				

Composition of American ryes, arranged by States.

State.	Serial number.	Water.	Ash.	Oil.	Carb-hydrates.	Fiber.	Albuminoids.	Nitrogen.
Vermont	5322	7.80	1.68	2.00	76.84	1.35	10.33	1.65
	5323	8.07	1.85	2.12	75.03	1.38	11.55	1.85
	5324	8.90	1.60	1.80	75.32	1.35	11.03	1.76
Connecticut	5024	8.84	2.00	1.91	75.02	1.38	10.85	1.74
	5027	7.74	2.20	2.09	75.72	1.75	10.50	1.68
	5028	9.17	1.97	1.74	75.55	1.32	10.25	1.62
	5029	9.69	1.88	1.80	75.38	1.45	9.80	1.57
Rhode Island	5290	9.75	2.10	1.71	74.40	1.89	10.15	1.62
New York	5223	3.02	2.55	2.09	71.43	1.38	14.53	2.32
	5225	9.12	2.40	1.58	74.96	1.26	10.68	1.71
	5231	8.98	2.16	1.69	74.37	1.25	11.55	1.85
	5234	8.93	1.77	2.10	76.42	1.33	9.45	1.51
	5235	7.35	2.16	2.13	75.37	1.61	11.38	1.32
New Jersey	5214	9.05	2.10	2.16	75.61	1.10	9.98	1.60
	5215	8.93	2.03	1.74	74.34	1.23	11.73	1.88
Pennsylvania	5282	9.35	2.15	1.86	73.71	1.20	11.73	1.88
	5286	8.75	2.14	1.76	74.63	1.34	11.38	1.82
	5286	9.35	1.70	1.92	74.31	1.52	11.20	1.79
Ohio	5260	9.81	2.55	1.79	74.00	1.35	10.50	1.68
	5269	8.15	1.70	1.93	74.26	1.88	12.08	1.93
Indiana	5086	9.60	1.57	1.73	77.22	1.13	8.75	1.40
Illinois	5060	9.57	1.93	2.16	74.59	1.42	10.33	1.65
	5062	9.99	3.72	1.98	72.41	1.35	10.55	1.68
	5063	8.85	1.80	2.09	76.01	1.10	10.15	1.62
	5066	7.62	2.73	2.06	72.68	1.95	12.96	2.07
	5067	8.85	2.15	1.85	75.05	1.25	10.85	1.74
	5068	8.73	3.37	1.86	71.33	1.58	13.13	2.10
	5070	9.45	1.60	1.92	75.08	1.45	10.50	1.68
	5075	8.45	2.36	1.98	72.48	1.60	13.13	2.10
	5079	9.18	1.62	1.70	75.15	1.15	11.20	1.79
Wisconsin	5351	8.65	2.32	1.86	74.50	1.47	11.20	1.79
	5353	8.41	1.55	1.59	76.97	1.15	10.33	1.65
	5357	8.80	1.96	1.84	74.50	1.35	11.55	1.85
	5360	8.38	1.90	1.38	74.88	1.56	11.90	1.90
	5361	10.00	1.95	1.69	74.13	1.38	10.85	1.74
Minnesota	5167	9.13	1.94	1.63	74.70	1.40	11.20	1.79
	5168	8.75	1.85	1.94	74.38	1.18	11.90	1.90
	5179	7.25	2.40	2.46	73.51	1.95	12.43	1.99
Iowa	5094	7.69	1.98	2.16	75.81	1.68	10.68	1.71
	5097	8.50	2.80	2.48	73.32	1.53	11.38	1.82
	5107	8.32	2.08	1.93	75.01	1.28	11.38	1.82
Missouri	5188	7.27	1.93	2.19	75.82	1.59	11.20	1.79
Nebraska	5198	8.27	1.31	2.25	77.54	1.39	9.28	1.48
Maryland	5140	9.70	2.10	1.93	73.16	1.38	11.73	1.88
	5141	9.64	1.80	1.65	74.63	1.43	10.85	1.74
Virginia	5334	8.60	2.30	1.77	73.10	1.80	12.43	1.99
West Virginia	5346	8.87	2.67	1.90	73.70	1.31	11.55	1.85
	5348	8.35	2.68	1.75	73.60	1.54	12.08	1.93
North Carolina	5248	8.75	2.01	1.85	74.46	1.55	11.38	1.82
	5250	8.60	1.55	2.33	74.64	1.63	12.25	1.96
South Carolina	5209	8.44	1.76	1.73	76.01	1.56	10.50	1.68
Kentucky	5116²			2.27		1.70	12.25	1.96
	5116	9.82	1.93	1.93	72.86	1.38	12.08	1.93
Georgia	5052	8.24	1.91	2.17	72.90	1.83	12.95	2.07
Colorado	3582	9.05	2.80	1.98	68.74	1.85	15.58	2.49
	3581	8.05	1.95	2.91	72.38	1.76	12.95	2.07
	5021	6.85	2.05	2.01	76.23	1.48	11.38	1.82
Washington Territory	5341	7.00	2.10	2.05	76.27	1.55	11.03	1.76

Average composition of American ryes, arranged by States.

State.	Number of analyses.	Water.	Ash.	Oil.	Carb-hydrates.	Fiber.	Albuminoids.	Nitrogen.
United States	57	8.67	2.09	1.94	74.52	1.46	11.32	1.81
Atlantic Slope	25	8.75	1.99	1.91	74.74	1.45	11.26	1.79
Northern States	43	8.73	2.08	1.92	74.74	1.43	11.10	1.79
Western States	25	8.71	2.12	1.94	74.82	1.44	11.17	1.79
Southern States	10	8.80	2.07	1.90	74.01	1.54	11.68	1.88
Pacific Slope	4	7.74	2.23	2.24	73.40	1.66	12.73	2.04
Vermont	3	8.26	1.71	1.97	75.73	1.36	10.97	1.75
Connecticut	4	8.86	2.01	1.88	75.44	1.48	10.33	1.65
Rhode Island	1	9.75	2.10	1.71	74.44	1.89	10.15	1.62
New York	5	8.48	2.21	1.92	74.51	1.36	11.52	1.84
New Jersey	2	8.99	2.06	1.95	74.98	1.16	10.86	1.74
Pennsylvania	3	9.15	1.99	1.85	74.22	1.35	11.44	1.83
Ohio	2	8.98	2.13	1.86	74.13	1.61	11.29	1.81
Indiana	1	9.60	1.57	1.73	77.22	1.13	8.75	1.40
Illinois	9	8.96	2.36	1.96	73.87	1.43	11.42	1.83
Wisconsin	5	8.85	1.94	1.67	74.99	1.38	11.17	1.79
Minnesota	3	8.36	2.06	2.01	74.20	1.51	11.84	1.89
Iowa	3	8.17	2.29	2.19	74.71	1.50	11.14	1.78
Missouri	1	7.27	1.93	2.19	75.82	1.59	11.20	1.79
Nebraska	1	8.27	1.31	2.25	77.54	1.35	9.28	1.48
Maryland	2	9.67	1.95	1.79	73.90	1.40	11.29	1.81
Virginia	1	8.60	2.30	1.77	73.10	1.80	12.43	1.99
West Virginia	2	8.61	2.67	1.83	73.65	1.42	11.82	1.89
North Carolina	2	8.17	1.78	2.09	74.55	1.59	11.62	1.89
South Carolina	1	8.44	1.76	1.73	76.01	1.56	10.50	1.68
Kentucky	1	9.82	1.93	1.93	72.86	1.38	12.08	1.93
Georgia	1	8.24	1.91	2.17	73.90	1.83	11.35	2.07
Colorado	3	7.98	2.24	2.30	72.45	1.70	13.20	2.13
Washington Territory	1	7.00	2.10	2.05	76.27	1.55	11.03	1.76

The largest specimen was from Washington Territory, weighing 3.450 grams, the next from Minnesota, weighing 2.780 per 100 grains, and the heaviest weight per bushel from Vermont, 64.1 pounds. The smallest were from Iowa and Nebraska, weighing 1.300 grams per hundred, and the lightest from New York, 56.2 pounds per bushel, the average for the country being 2.074 and 60.9. The largest and heaviest ryes were found on the Atlantic coast and in the Northern States. The Pacific slope was not well represented.

The average weight per bushel is much higher than is usually accepted for rye, but the specimens in hand certainly reached those figures perhaps being very clean or selected samples above the average production. Illinois, which in the last census year produced more of the crop than any State except New York, sends the smallest and the lightest average grain.

In chemical composition the following extremes were found:

	Highest.	State.	Lowest.	State.
	Per cent.		Per cent.	
Water	10.00	Wisconsin	7.00	Washington Territory.
Ash	3.72	Illinois	1.31	Nebraska.
Oil	2.91	Colorado	1.38	Wisconsin.
Carbhydrates	77.54	Nebraska	68.74	Colorado.
Crude fiber	1.90	Minnesota	1.10	Illinois.
Albuminoids	15.58	Colorado	8.75	Indiana.

But 5 were below 10 per cent. of albuminoids, and all but 4 were below 13 per cent.

The grain cannot be said to be extremely variable. The averages for the country is here given, together with an average of 49 analyses of ryes from all sources given by Koenig:

	United States.	Koenig.
Water	8.67	15.06
Ash	2.09	1.89
Oil	1.94	1.79
Carbhydrates	74.52	67.81
Crude fiber	1.46	2.01
Albuminoids	11.32	11.52

The extremes of albuminoid in Koenig's analyses were 16.93 and 7.91 per cent., which is wider than among our specimens. The difference between our grain and that of the Continent appears in the greater moisture of the latter, as is to be expected, together with more ash and oil and less fiber. For different parts of the United States the averages are very nearly concordant, the only variation being the difference of half a per cent. albuminoids and a little more fiber in ten specimens from the South. The nitrogenous constituents are practically the same. This cereal is richer than corn in this element, and not quite so rich as wheat.

Rye cannot be considered as being very susceptible to climatic conditions; in fact, it will flourish where other cereals will not. It requires therefore no greater care in its improvement than the selection of the variety giving the largest yield, and careful cultivation.

BARLEY.

Of American barley, from any point of view, but little has been known hitherto. Until lately, only nine chemical anaylses have been made, and, as Professor Brewer remarks, these are too few in number for generalizations. Statistics show that we have not produced enough of the cereal to supply the demand, and that it is always necessary to import a large amount every year. A study, therefore, of the conditions which affect the production of barley in the United States, which portions produce the most valuable grain, and how the composition varies in different localities as the result of climate and general environment, will be of interest, as showing the possibilities and best localities for the extension of the growth of this cereal.

Before discussing the results of our examination of the numerous American specimens collected through our agents, it will be of interest to give abstracts of some investigations on the production of barley in certain portions of Germany and this country, showing the yield, weight, physical characters and composition, and the directions in which it is considered desirable that this grain should be developed.

Dr. Maercker, of Halle, in a report on "Barley Experiments with Seed from Various Sources," a copy of which he has been good enough to send us, says that the problem of the production of the best barley has become an important one in the last few years in the province of the Salle, which has heretofore produced the best quality, but recently has met with much ill luck. To the end of studying the conditions affecting this cereal and learning the physical and chemical characteristics of the best varieties, seed selected by a mixed jury from a large exhibition of barleys were devoted to the experiment, and distributed among the leading agriculturists of the province. The varieties were grown with different supplies of nitrogenous manures, all the seed having been judged extremely fine (hochfein), and found to possess the following characteristics:

	Albuminoids.	Mealy kernels.
	Per cent.	Per cent.
Slavonian	7.7	92
Mravian	7.7	90
Danish	7.7	90
Saalish	8.1	80

From the experiments it was found that in the matter of yield the higher was obtained with the larger supply of nitrogenous manure, but that the quality was somewhat injured thereby, as the percentage of albuminoids was considerably raised, as can be seen from the determinations which were made:

	Saalish.	Danish.	Moravian.	Slavonian.
Original seed	8.10	7.70	7.70	7.70
100 kilograms Chili saltpeter, per hectare	8.19	9.16	9.18	8.92
200 kilograms Chili saltpeter, per hectare	8.48	9.56	9.78	9.52

The quality or consistency of the original seed was found in most cases to be lowered; and although the Slowakisch barley was superior to the rest, three samples out of seventeen being extremely fine, three fine, and eight good, it was nevertheless apparent that although the quality of the seed is an essential factor in the quality of the harvest, it is not the only one, but that climate, soil, manuring, and cultivation are much more important and of greater influence. One can in no way expect that the production of barley can be improved by selected seed alone. Care in other directions and favorable climatic influences, over which we have no control, are necessary as well.

The heavy manuring of nitrogenous material, as has been said, injured the quality, and how much so in comparison with a light one can be seen by enumerating the number of experimental samples which were found to be below the mean in quality. Of 89 manured with 100 kilograms of Chili saltpeter per hectare, only 6 were below medium; of

78 having 200 kilograms per hectare, 16 were below medium. Nitrogenous manures are not, accordingly, to be considered advisable on barley.

As to the relation of percentage of albuminoids, weight per bushel, and consistency to the quality of the grain, Dr. Mäercker remarks:

For a long time the author has busied himself with the question whether the amount of albuminoids stood in any relation to the value of barley, and in many cases this question could be answered that with few exceptions a barley rich in albuminoids is of poor quality, while a low content of albuminoids in general was an expression of high quality. It is, of course, understood that exterior conditions, rain, moisture, &c., can injure their value and make the barleys of low albuminoids of less worth than others richer in nitrogen. In proof of this, the decisions of the judges and the testimony of the laboratory furnish all that is desired.

The albuminoids in the crop as given in the previous table were over 1 per cent. higher than in the seed, and the quality was adjudged correspondingly poorer, and the specimen considered to be the worst was found to have increased 2.08 per cent. over the seed. Comparing the decision of the judges with the percentages of albuminoids the following coincidence was found:

Specimens denominated—	Mean per cent. of albuminoids.
Extremely fine	8.09
Fine	8.67
Good	8.93
Medium	9.78
Under medium	10.24

From these figures it cannot be denied "that high content of albuminoids appears to be incompatible with high quality."

To the weight the judges paid little attention. The determinations showed no relation between quality and weight.

Weight per hectoliter in kilograms * of the seed was as follows:

	Per cent.
Slavonian	68.7
Moravian	70.8
Danish	69.0
Saalish	69.2

And of the crops in the mean:

	Saalish.	Danish.	Moravian.	Slavonian.
100 kilograms saltpeter	67.2	67.2	66.6	67.3
200 kilograms saltpeter	67.2	66.8	67.5	66.7
Mean	67.1	67.0	67.1	67.0
Less than seed	2.1	2.0	3.7	1.7

The weight of the crop is on the average less than the seed; but between the different varieties there is no difference in the mean weight, despite the fact that there is a difference in quality.

* Kilogram per hectoliter × .7752 = pounds per bushel.

In regard to the mealy consistency of the grain the following figures furnish an explanation:

Per cent. of mealy kernels.

	Saalish.	Danish.	Moravian	Slavonian.
	Per cent.	Per cent.	Per cent.	Per cent.
Seed	80.0	90.0	90.0	92.0
100 kilograms saltpeter	62.4	70.1	68.7	77.5
200 kilograms saltpeter	64.9	65.9	66.8	64.7
Mean	63.7	68.0	67.8	71.1
Less than seed	16.3	22.0	22.2	20.9

The mealiness of the crop is much less than of the seed, which agrees again with the decision of the judges, who it may be remarked placed the greatest dependence on the consistency of the kernel in forming their opinion, and in other respects with the conclusions derived from other characteristics.

Among a collection of 50 barleys which were submitted with the experimental specimens already mentioned, there were found none worthy of mention except the crop of one gentleman who had used no nitrogen but heavy manuring with phosphoric acid. His barleys were graded as follows:

	Extra fine (a).	Extra fine (b).	Extra fine (c).	Extra fine (d).	Fine.
	Per cent.	Per cent.	Per cent.	Per cent.	Per cent.
Albumen	8.8	7.9	7.7	8.4	8.2
Weight	70.0	69.1	68.1	70.3	67.3
Mealy	88.0	88.0	82.0	86.0	86.0

From the preceding experiments we learn that the characteristics of a first quality barley are its consistency, color, and its albuminoid percentage, the latter in fine barleys not exceeding 8.67.

Several other investigators in previous years have not found the average up to the standard which has been set by the judges just mentioned. The results of Reischauer[*] show that the barleys which he had in hand were somewhat richer in nitrogen than those of Mäercker.

In 100 parts of dry substance.

	Nitrogen.	N × 6.25 Albuminoids.	Ash.	Phosphoric acid.	Silica.	Iron oxide.	Lime.
	Per cent.	Per cent.	Per cent.	Per cent.	Per cent.	Per cent.	Per cent.
Maximum	2.856	17.85	3.34	1.145	0.845	0.0694	0.151
Minimum	1.282	8.01	2.12	0.614	0.460	0.0019	0.043
Average	1.729	10.804	2.799	0.902	0.641	0.0200	0.068

[*] Zeitschrift für das gesamte Brauwesen, 353–363; Bied. Centralblatt 11, 42–43.

In 100 *parts of dry substance*—Continued.

Source of barley.	Nitrogen.	N × 6.25 Albuminoid.	Ash.	Phosphoric acid.
Austria	1.564	9.77	2.818	0.900
Bavaria	1.655	10.34	2.848	0.944
Wurtemberg	1.658	10.36	2.860	0.962
Hesse	1.750	10.93	2.923	1.019
Prussia	1.806	11.29	2.853	0.920
Sweden	2.121	12.36	2.515	0.841
Denmark	1.661	10.38	2.720	0.928
Russia	2.188	13.67	2.753	0.921
Alsace	1.609	10.62	2.802	0.880
France	1.769	11.05	2.936	0.897
Africa	1.833	11.46	2.730	0.781

Louis Marx has also examined a large number of barleys—four hundred—from various countries, extending over six years' crops. His results have furnished the following averages for the amount of albuminoids usually present:

Series.	Source.	Mean.
		Per cent.
First series	(1) Russia	12.76
	(2) Baden	12.38
	(3) Sweden	11.97
	(4) Danube Province	11.68
	(5) Brunswick	11.49
Second series	(6) North Germany { Potsdam, 12.21; Oderbruch, 11.93; Magdeburg, 11.28; Saal, 10.49. }	11.21
	(7) Bavaria	10.76
	(8) Alsace	10.70
	(9) Hungary	10.62
Third series	(10) France { Champagne, 10.90; Bourgoigne, 10.86; Auvergne, 9.90 }	10.55
	(11) Hesse	10.43
	(12) Wurtemberg	10.38
	(13) Denmark	10.91
	(14) England	9.69
Fourth series	(15) Austria { Slavonia, 9.90; Moravia, 9.79; Bohemia 9.12 }	9.61

In Russia, as with wheats, barley was found to be rich in albuminoids, one reaching 16.00. Bohemia and England, both celebrated for their malt, furnished but few samples with over 10.00 per cent. Bavaria, with 68 samples, had only 6 over 12.00 per cent.

The thick-hulled barleys were as a whole poorer in nitrogen, the hull being, of course, poor in that element. There was found to be no relation between nitrogen and phosphoric acid.

Some analyses by Lunter of barleys of the crop of 1883, used in the experimental brewery at Munich, have been published lately in Biedermann's Centralblatt für Agrikulturchemie, without great comment.

He finds in the experimental field that continuous cultivation for years can be carried on without essential alteration of the quality.

Serial number.	Source of barley.	Dry substances.					
		Nitrogen.	Albuminoids.	Phosphoric acid.	Starch.	Water.	Germinability.
		Per cent.	Per cent.	Per cent.	Per cent.	Per cent.	Per cent.
1	Erding	1.646	10.29	1.003	71.28	8.46	30.80
2	Unterfranken	1.806	11.29	0.931	59.62	17.84	88.60
3	Bayer Landegerstel	1.661	10.38	1.047	66.45	16.58	90.10
4	Franken	1.601	10.00	0.913	66.61	14.82	95.40
5	Freisinger Gerstel	1.623	11.14	0.951	65.84	12.28	80.15
6	Moosburger	1.585	9.90	0.930	65.16	12.47	83.14
7	Langenbacher	1.680	10.50	0.935	65.82	12.67	90.00
8	Landshuter	1.722	10.76	1.034	64.18	13.26	89.20

These samples, in albuminoids, certainly do not attain the high standard of quality set by Maercker.

Of American barleys, the only investigation, in addition to nine analyses collected by Professor Brewer, is that of eleven specimens at the Brewers' Experiment Station in New York, in 1883 or 1884,* the results of which are here given in one hundred parts of dry substance:

Serial number.	Source.	Weight per bushel.	Water.	Dry substance.	Dry substance.			
					Starch.	Albuminoid (N. × 6.25).	Ash.	Phosphoric acid.
		Lbs.	Per cent.	Per cent.	Per cent.	Per cent.	Per cent.	Per cent.
1	Canada	50¼	10.04	89.96	63.63	10.73	2.78	0.950
2	Iowa	48¾	9.22	90.78	59.48	11.18	3.16	1.149
3	Bald barley (Kansas)	57½	10.41	89.59	64.49	10.16	2.86	0.997
4	Western barley	48¼	9.56	90.44	60.30	12.39	3.21	1.124
5	......do	48¾	9.36	90.64	61.36	11.36	3.31	1.278
6	Scotch barley (Waukesha County, Wis.)	48	10.21	89.79	59.54	8.18	3.77	1.582
7	New York State		12.05	87.95	66.31	12.79	2.59	
8	California	54	12.40	87.60	66.54	13.60	2.45	
9	Wisconsin barley	48¼	11.89	88.11	65.98	10.27	2.84	1.000
10	Wisconsin barley (Farmer barley)	47	11.56	88.44	66.29	12.23	2.96	1.030
11	New York State	50	14.06	85.94	63.70	11.62	2.51	
	Mean	50¼	10.96	89.04	63.42	11.32	2.95	1.139

The investigation proves principally that the weight per bushel is hardly a safe guide as to quality, but one must rather judge from the percentage of moisture and nitrogenous constituents which the grain contains. The specimens examined were certainly not extremely starchy, nor were they very dry. Being so few in number, they hardly form a basis for rational conclusion in regard to our grain and its comparison with that of other countries, but they were considered by the editor of the Prag. Agricultural Journal as showing that American barleys were quite equal to those of the Continent.

* Bied. Centbl. j. Agrikchemie 13, 491–2.

The results which have been quoted, while showing that the standard to be reached if possible is a large mealy grain with not more than 8 per cent. of albuminoids as described by Maercker, seem to prove rather conclusively that little barely of this quality is produced on the Continent or elsewhere. The best ranges in the neighborhood of 9.5 per cent. and from 10 to 11 is a fair average.

The sixty samples from all parts of the United States and twelve from Canada, collected for the present investigation, will, when examined in connection with the previous results at home and abroad, give us a reasonable basis for deciding as to our shortcomings and peculiarities.

AMERICAN BARLEY.

The samples of American barley have been collected through our agents from those parts of the country where it is a crop of prominence. They represent fairly well the production of the United States. The largest number of analyses are not for the largest areas of production—New York, Wisconsin, and California, which raise more than half the crop—but they are scattered through all the States where any amount of barley is grown. In considering the average features of the crop as it is found in market, regard must be had especially for the figures for Canada and the three States named, although the California barley never reaches our Eastern markets.

The other cereals have been analyzed free from any hulls or chaff. It would have been of interest for comparison to have been able to separate the barleys in the same way. Owing to the close adherence this is very difficult, but in a few cases it was attempted and the analyses of these specimens are given, together with a few of the naked varieties.

The sources of the barleys are described in the following tables.

65

Sources of specimens of barley.

State.	Serial number.	Name.	When sown.	When reaped.	County.	Post-office.	Sender.	Remarks.
California	4015	Coast	Feb. 1	June 1	Ventura	New Jerusalem	M. McLaughlin	
	4016	Six-rowed	Feb. to Mar	July	Contra Costa	Martinez	J. Strentzel	Brown.
Connecticut	4038	Two-rowed	Apr. 28	Aug. 4 to 8	Litchfield	West Cornwall	T. S. Gold	
Dakota	4030	Common	May 5	July 20	Stutsman	Jamestown	J. S. Nichols	
	4035	Chevalier	May 3	July 25	Cass	Fargo	W. H. Leverett	
Illinois	4030	Four-rowed	Apr. 1 to 15	July 15 to 20	Bon Homme	Tyndall	A. Ziencot	Brown.
	4002	Common	Apr.	July 15	Stephenson	Howardsville	A. M. Durkee	Seed from Department.
	4003	Common spring	Early April	do	Ogle	Baileyville	W. B. Derrick	Brown.
	4063	Spring			McHenry	Crystal Lake	James Crow	Not first quality. Forty-eight bushels per acre.
Indiana	4067	Common	Mar. to Apr	July 1 to 16	Lee	Dixon	Abram Brown	White, mealy.
	4080	...do	Sept. 10 to 20	June 10 to 20	Shelby	Morristown	W. W. Woodward	Do.
	4081	Early May	Last Aug. to Sept	June 1 to 15	Franklin	Mount Carmel	J. A. Applegate	
	4085	Do not know	Sept. to Oct. 15	Last of May	Spencer	Rockport	James Lane	
Iowa	4090							
	4091	Scotch	Apr. 1	July 4	Scott	Davenport	H. C. Fulton	
	4097	Quinlau	Mar 25 to Apr. 10	July 25 to Aug. 10	Sac	Wall Lake	J. H. Hoebing	
	4098	Four-rowed	Apr. 10 to 15	July 15 to 20	Palo Alto	Ruthven	J. A. Anthony	Fifteen-year grown.
	4101	Common	Apr. 15	July 15	Winneshiek	Decorah	M. H. Merrill	Brown.
	4104	...do	Apr.	July 25	Fayette	West Union	B. F. Conkey	Do.
	4107	Spring	Apr. 1 to 15	July 20	Clinton	Bryant	D. Conrad	
Kentucky	4122	Canada	Sept. 26	June 20	Jefferson	Fern Creek	N. Cartwright	
Michigan	4151	Four-rowed	Apr. 10	July 15	Genesee	Flint	F. H. Rankin	
	4153	Six-rowed	March 27	July 28	Livingston	Highland	J. D. Cronse	
	4156	Common	Apr. 21	Aug. 1	Ottawa	Berlin	C. W. Wilde	
	4158	Four-rowed	Apr. 26	July 28	Saint Clair	Jeddo	Moses Locke	
	4160	...do	Apr. 20	July 25	Shiawassee	Corunna	S. R. Kelsey	Brown.
Minnesota	4163				Todd	Long Prairie	L. S. Hendley	
	4166	Spring	Middle May	Aug. 12	Otter Tail	Deer Creek	C. E. Mason	
	4169	Three-rowed	May 20	July 20	Dodge	Mantorville	Z. B. Page	
	4170	Scotch			Winona	Minnesota City	O. M. Lord	Brown.
	4172	...do	May 8	July 27	Dakota	Hastings	R. A. Simmons	
	4175	Four-rowed	Apr. 23	July 15	Blue Earth	Willow Creek	E. P. Wilder	Bleached with rain.
	4176	Scotch	Apr. 24	July 20	Olmsted	Marion	A. J. Grode	Brown.
	4170	...do	May 5	Aug. 1	Fillmore	Fillmore	G. W. Knight	Do.
Missouri	4188		Apr. 1 to 20	June 15 to 25	Atchison	Langdon	R. Buckham	
Montana	4196	Common two-rowed	Apr. 15	Last of August	Meagher	Canton	J. G. Pickering	
Nebraska	4197	Two-rowed or English	May 1	Aug. 15	Gallatin	Bozeman	William Flannery	Do.
Nevada	4198	Common six-rowed	Apr. 1	July 1 to 10	Antelope	Neleigh	F. H. Trowbridge	
	4202	...do	Apr. 2	Aug. 14	Esmeralda	Wellington	T. B. Smith	
	4205	Lincoln	Apr. 15	October	Douglas	Genoa	H. F. Dangberg	
New York	4220	(?)	(?)	(?)	Yates	Nile Centre	A. H. Ansley	
	4228	Five-rowd barley	June 3	Aug. 27	Alleguny	Nile	Jesse D. Rogers	

13734—No. 9——5

Sources of specimens of barley—Continued.

State.	Serial number.	Name.	When sown.	When reaped.	County.	Post-office.	Sender.	Remarks.
New York	4232	Canada six rowed	May 1 to 15	July 1 to 15	Ontario	Naples	J. M. Anable	Mealy, white.
	4223	Canada two rowed	May 1	Aug. 8	Otsego	Cooperstown	G. P. Kness	
	4235	Imperial	May 1	Aug. 1	Schoharie	Schoharie	I. C. Van Tuyl	
	4243	Imperial six-rowel	Apr. 20	Aug. 1	Cayuga	Fleming	Howard Tryon	
Ohio	4260	Early, May	Sept. 10 to 25	June 1 to 10	Butler	Gano	Joseph Allen	Brown.
	4200	Fall	Oct. 8	June 20	Wood	Mermill	Andrew Welton	
Oregon	4271	Chevalier		Aug. 15	Warren	Lebanon	D. P. Egbert	Brown.
	4275		Apr. 1 May	Aug. to Sept.	Baker	Baker City	Thomas Smith	
	4277		Feb. 5, to May		Linn	Albany	G. F. Crawford	
	4423				Grant	Canyon City		
Pennsylvania	4285	Nohama	May 10	July 15	Crawford	Conneautville	R. Bolard	For early feed.
South Carolina	4290	Four-rowed	October	Last of May	Laurens	Goolgion's Factory	J. S. Wolf	
Utah	4319	Two-rowed	May 1	Sept. 1	Wasatch	Heber	John Crook	
Vermont	4321	Four-rowed	May 8	(?)	Windsor	Pomfret	Crosby Miller	
	4324	do	May 15 to July 1	Aug. 15 to Sept. 20	Washington	Montpelier	A. D. Arms	
	4328	Common	May 10	Aug. 15	Orleans	Irasburgh	Z. E. Jameson	
Wisconsin	4351	Common	May 15	July 15	Chippewa	Eagle Point	John Datre	Brown.
	4353	(?)	(?)	(?)	Vernon	Viroqua	William Cox.	Do.
	4357	(?)	(?)		La Fayette	La Fayette	S. E. Roberts	Do.
	4360	Scotch Pearl	Apr. 17	July 27	Fond du Lac	Metomen	E. Reynolds	Do.
	4361	Mensury	May 1 to 5	July 25	Dodge	Burnett	H. Sawyer	
	4364	Common	December	June	Pinal	Florence	W. E. Guild.	
Arizona	4374	(?)		(?)	Solano		H. Peters	
California	4378		Jan. to March	June to July	Monterey	Salinas	J. R. Leese	
Dakota	4390	Common	Mar. 1	Late August	Humboldt	Eureka	Fred Axe.	
	4362	(?)	(?)	(?)	Traill	Caledonia	P. Hebrandson	
	4301	(?)	(?)	(?)	Lawrence	Deadwood	J. Carney.	
Michigan	4406	Common	May 10	Aug. 20	Cheboygan	Cheboygan	Jacob Walker	
Montana	4415	Two-rowed brewers	Apr. 15 to May 10	Aug. 15	Deer Lodge	Deer Lodge City	D. C. Irvine	
	4423	Bald	Apr. 18	July 30	Grant	John Day City	Joseph Magone	
	4423ª	Common	do	do	do	do	do	
Washington	4435	Black Nepaul	Fall or spring	Early or late summer.	Pierce	Tacoma	L. E. Sampson	Brown.
Ohio	4444	Common Fall	Sept. 1 to 15	June 1 to 20	Butler	Hamilton	G. K. Shaffer	
Iowa	4445	(?)			Lyon	Larchwood	J. B. Warren	

CANADIAN BARLEYS.

The specimens of Canadian barleys were obtained by application to Hon. A. Blue, of the Bureau of Agriculture and Arts, in Toronto. He forwarded them to the Department with the following letter:

> I was not able until yesterday to get the samples of Ontario barley asked for by you for analysis. They were sent on by express, and I trust will reach you safely. The samples have been collected from four districts of the Province, and graded 1, 2, and 3 by the Government inspector here. The districts are indicated as A, B, C, and D, and the localities are shown on the inclosed map.
>
> As a rule, our best barley is produced in the counties north of Lake Ontario, and especially in those bordering on the Bay of Quinte, viz, Prince Edward, Lennox, and Addington and Hastings; but this year it was injured there by rains at the harvest season.
>
> The western district is much more subject to summer rains, owing to its situation between the Great Lakes, and the barley is often discolored.
>
> The brightest grain this year is found in the counties of Peel, York, Ontario, and Durham.
>
> I shall be greatly obliged if you will send me the results of your analysis.

The districts as indicated included—

A, the counties north of the central part of Lake Erie; B, the counties north of the northwestern part of Lake Ontario; C, the counties north of the central portion of Lake Ontario; D, the counties north of the northeastern portion of Lake Ontario, bordering on the Bay of Quinte.

B, C, and D are therefore the best barleys, and especially D, which was, however, unfortunately injured this year, and the brightest grain found in B.

How these practical opinions of quality agree with the facts learned from chemical analysis and with the investigations of Maercker will appear in our discussion of the results.

CHEMICAL AND PHYSICAL DATA.

In the following tables are arranged the data which have been obtained from an examination of the specimens which have been described, together with averages for the United States and Canada, and for the various States and geographical divisions:

Canadian barleys.

Grade.	Serial number.	District.	Composition.							Weight.		Consistency.			
			Water.	Ash.	Oil.	Carbohydrates.	Fiber.	Albuminoids.	Nitrogen.	Weight per 100 grains.	Weight per bushel.	Mealy.	Half mealy.	Quartermealy.	Little mealy.	Glassy.
			P. ct.	P. ct.	P. ct.	P. ct.	P. ct.	P. ct.	P. c.	Grms.	Lbs.					
First quality	6041	A¹	7.58	2.98	2.70	73.49	3.10	10.15	1.62	2.910	54.8	16	32	24	20	8
Do	6044	B¹	8.35	2.73	2.69	73.23	3.55	9.45	1.51	3.060	56.1	..	48	36	12	4
Do	6047	C¹	6.95	2.68	2.64	74.28	3.65	9.80	1.57	3.206	55.9	40	28	20	12	..
Do	6050	D¹	8.35	2.88	2.67	73.13	3.69	9.28	1.48	3.445	52.7	12	36	36	16	..
Average			7.81	2.82	2.67	73.53	3.50	9.67	1.54	3.158	54.9	17	36	29	15	3
Second quality	6042	A²	7.85	2.95	2.72	72.76	3.22	10.50	1.68	2.818	54.5	36	40	12	12	..
Do	6045	B²	7.03	2.80	2.80	73.46	3.76	10.15	1.62	3.056	54.7	16	36	28	16	4
Do	6048	C²	10.08	1.62	2.78	72.58	3.49	9.45	1.51	2.934	53.5	12	36	32	20	..
Do	6051	D²	8.43	3.18	2.63	72.55	3.41	9.80	1.57	3.257	53.5	24	40	32	4	..
Average			8.35	2.64	2.73	72.84	3.47	9.97	1.59	3.021	54.1	22	38	26	13	1
Third quality	6043	A³	8.78	2.70	2.69	72.35	3.50	9.98	1.60	3.012	52.4	36	28	24	8	4
Do	6046	B²	6.75	2.83	2.72	73.87	3.68	10.15	1.62	3.094	54.8	16	44	32	..	8
Do	6049	C³	8.13	3.05	2.67	72.82	3.35	9.98	1.60	2.941	52.4	..	40	44	16	..
Do	6052	D³	7.03	3.18	2.74	73.47	3.35	9.33	1.40	3.226	54.3	20	32	24	20	4
Average			7.89	2.94	2.71	73.13	3.47	9.86	1.58	3.068	53.5	18	36	31	11	4
Average A locality			8.07	2.88	2.70	72.87	3.27	10.21	1.63	2.943	53.9	30	33	20	13	4
Average B locality			7.37	2.79	2.74	73.52	3.66	9.92	1.58	3.073	55.2	11	43	32	9	5
Average C locality			8.39	2.45	2.70	73.23	3.49	9.74	1.56	3.027	53.9	17	35	32	16	..
Average D locality			8.24	3.08	2.68	73.05	3.48	9.47	1.51	3.309	53.5	19	36	31	13	1
Grand average			8.02	2.80	2.70	73.17	3.48	9.83	1.57	3.088	54.1	19	37	29	13	2

Physical properties of barley.

Locality.	Serial No.	Weight of 100 grains.	Weight per bushel.	Mealy.	Half mealy.	Quartermealy.	Little mealy.	Glassy.
Vermont	4323	3.120	52.2		16	44	24	16
	4324	3.480	51.4	40	36	16	8	
	4326	2.980	52.4		20	40	40	
Connecticut	4028	4.380	53.0	12	24	36	28	
New York	4220	3.390	57.7					
	4226	2.880	54.5					
	4228	3.300	51.4		36	44	20	
	4232	3.570	53.4	16	28	28	28	
	4233	3.380	49.3	20	40	28	12	
	4235		51.0					
	4243 I	3.410	54.7	8	24	24	44	
	4243 II	2.690	52.9					
Pennsylvania	4285	2.630	50.4	8	36	24	32	
Ohio	4260	3.690	53.9	16	40	32	12	
	4269	3.170	50.8	36	36	20	8	
	4271	3.180	52.5	40	44	12	4	
	4444	2.980	51.0	40	32	20	8	
Michigan	4151	3.450	54.3	16	36	40	8	
	4153	2.280	49.3		32	36	24	8
	4156	3.200	51.3	24	28	28	20	
	4158	3.260	56.8	4	36	44	16	
	4160	3.180	53.7	16	40	28	16	
	4406	3.530	58.7	24	32	28	16	
Indiana	4080	3.310	53.2	24	48	28		
	4081	3.110	53.1	12	36	28	24	
	4085	3.570	54.3	48	22	16	14	
Illinois	4062	2.740	50.4	32	28	20	20	
	4063	2.840	49.8	28	32	32	8	
	4065	3.050	52.0	24	36	24	16	
	4066	2.880						
	4067	2.920	52.2	12	28	24	36	

Physical properties of barleys—Continued.

Locality.	Soriel No.	Weight of 100 grains.	Weight per bushel.	Mealy.	Half mealy.	Quarter mealy.	Little mealy.	Glassy.
Wisconsin	4351	3.180	50.6	8	32	40	20	
	4353	3.360	50.6	36	32	32		
	4357	2.930	48.5	36	24	24	16	
	4360	3.390	53.3	16	36	28	12	8
	4361	3.720	53.3	16	28	28	20	8
Minnesota	4163	3.610						
	4166	3.503	56.2	12	44	22	12	
	4169	2.610	50.8	16	36	36	12	
	4170	3.520	52.8	24	44	28	4	
	4172	3.390	50.8	40	36	24		
	4175	2.760	51.8	12	44	40	4	
	4176	3.220	51.8	28	36	28	8	
	4179	3.710	55.0	24	60	16		
Iowa	4090	2.820	53.5	16	52	24	8	
	4091	3.130	52.6	16	36	28	20	
	4097	2.900	51.4	24	36	28	12	
	4098	3.010	51.3	20	36	28	16	
	4101	2.890	54.8	8	20	32	32	8
	4104	3.320	55.3	8	32	44	16	
	4107	3.140	54.1	24	24	36	16	
Missouri	4188	2.642	53.1	12	28	52	8	
Nebraska	4198	3.830	53.2	4	28	40	28	
Dakota	4030	3.370	54.3	8	40	36	16	
	4035	4.930	56.7	16	32	40	12	
	4036	2.780	53.0	20	36	32	8	4
	4090	2.720	52.0	16	52	24	8	
	4091	3.000		16	36	28	20	
Montana	4196	3.950	58.6					
	4197	4.360	58.1	40	28	24	8	
	4415	4.350	57.4	76	24			
	4423		67.9					
	4423II		53.4	20	32	28	20	
South Carolina	4299	2.950						
Kentucky	4122	3.366						
Utah	4319	4.218	60.2	24	44	28	4	
Nevada	4202	4.290	55.1					
	4205	4.140	56.2					
Arizona	4364	4.180	53.2	20	44	28	8	
Washington Territory	4435	4.930	65.8	16	28	36	20	
Oregon	4275	4.490	59.9		24	40	36	
	4277	5.110	52.2	24	36	40		
California	4015	4.220	49.9	48	36	16		
	4016	4.920	55.7	24	48	20	8	
	4374	4.550	53.5	24	52	24		
	4378	5.180		8	48	32	12	
	4382	5.630						

Average physical properties of American barleys.

State.	No. of determinations.	Weight per 100 grains.	Weight per bushel.	Mealy.	Half mealy.	Quarter mealy.	Little mealy.	Glassy.
		Grams.	*Pounds.*					
United States	76	3.482	54.0	20	35	29	15	1
Canada	12	3.088	54.1	19	37	29	13	2
Eastern States	13	3.016	52.6	11	29	32	26	2
Western States	39	3.171	52.8	21	35	30	13	1
Northwestern States	10	3.680	57.2	27	35	26	11	1
Pacific Slope	12	4.655	56.8	21	40	29	10	0
Vermont	3	3.193	52.0	13	24	34	24	5
New York	8	3.217	53.1	11	32	31	26	0
Ohio	4	3.230	52.1	33	38	21	8	0
Michigan	6	3.150	54.0	14	34	34	16	1
Indiana	3	3.330	53.5	28	35	24	13	0
Illinois	5	2.890	51.1	28	32	25	15	0
Wisconsin	5	3.320	51.3	22	30	31	14	3
Minnesota	7	3.200	52.7	22	43	29	6	0
Iowa	7	3.030	53.4	17	34	32	16	1
Dakota	5	3.354	54.2	15	39	32	13	1
Montana	5	4.220	59.1	45	28	17	10	0
Nevada	2	4.215	55.7					0
Oregon	2	4.800	56.1	12	30	40	18	0
California	5	4.900	53.0	26	46	23	5	0

Composition of American barleys (unhulled), arranged by States.

State.	Serial No.	Water.	Ash.	Oil.	Carbhy-drates.	Fiber.	Albumi-noids.	Nitrogen.
		Per ct.	Per ct.	Per ct.	Per ct.	Per ct.	Per ct.	Per ct.
Vermont	4323	6.70	2.22	2.00	70.28	3.90	14.00	2.24
	4324	6.50	2.40	2.65	72.37	3.48	12.60	2.02
	4326	6.55	2.90	2.75	71.57	4.15	12.08	1.93
Connecticut	4028	6.50	2.99	2.33	75.14	2.89	10.15	1.62
New York	4226	6.86	2.40	2.76	72.85	3.40	11.73	1.88
	4228	6.77	2.12	2.77	73.41	3.55	11.38	1.82
	4232	5.90	2.70	2.58	74.14	3.05	11.03	1.76
	4233	6.95	2.64	2.66	74.47	3.13	10.15	1.62
	4243	7.39	2.45	2.48	73.10	3.73	10.85	1.74
Pennsylvania	4275	6.27	3.05	2.06	72.89	3.83	11.90	1.90
Ohio	4260	6.85	3.30	3.53	71.84	3.80	10.68	1.71
	4269	6.25	3.07	2.40	73.13	4.65	10.50	1.68
	4271	6.81	3.55	2.58	72.91	4.00	10.15	1.62
	4444	6.80	3.10	2.06	73.92	4.32	9.80	1.57
Michigan	4151	6.44	2.97	2.70	71.33	3.43	13.13	2.10
	4153	6.37	2.50	2.73	69.73	3.88	14.70	2.35
	4158	6.73	2.56	2.90	71.83	3.03	12.95	2.07
	4160	5.27	3.05	2.71	73.36	3.71	11.90	1.90
	4406	6.55	2.75	2.55	75.45	3.07	9.63	1.54
Indiana	4080	5.99	3.50	3.54	71.19	4.40	11.38	1.82
	4085	5.92	2.95	2.73	75.37	3.58	9.45	1.51
Illinois	4062	6.06	3.34	2.61	70.88	4.51	12.60	2.02
	4063	6.18	3.16	2.50	72.55	4.14	11.38	1.82
	4005	6.72	2.73	2.81	72.15	2.64	12.95	2.07
	4067	6.52	3.08	2.66	71.77	3.37	12.60	2.02
Wisconsin	4351	7.15	2.90	2.76	70.51	4.43	12.25	1.96
	4353	7.40	2.30	2.74	73.17	3.83	10.50	1.68
	4357	6.60	3.60	2.65	72.03	4.27	10.85	1.74
	4360	7.70	2.75	2.50	72.77	3.78	10.50	1.68
	4361	6.40	3.15	2.49	70.88	3.95	13.13	2.10
Minnesota	4169	7.60	1.50	2.60	73.79	3.57	10.85	1.74
	4170	6.20	3.00	3.07	73.88	4.40	9.45	1.51
	4172	6.30	2.51	2.76	74.72	4.43	9.28	1.48
	4175	7.22	3.15	2.80	71.25	3.08	11.90	1.90
	4176	9.15	2.97	2.72	70.69	3.97	10.50	1.68
Iowa	4091	6.47	2.85	2.63	71.34	3.93	12.73	2.04
	4098	5.60	3.18	2.75	72.28	4.37	11.73	1.88
	4101	6.24	2.97	2.83	72.68	3.00	11.38	1.82
	4104	6.67	3.33	2.65	69.19	3.81	14.35	2.30
Nebraska	4108	7.58	3.00	2.70	71.12	3.35	12.25	1.96
Dakota	4030	5.80	3.05	3.01	69.07	3.29	14.88	2.38
	4035	5.55	2.90	2.46	74.19	3.35	11.55	1.85
	4036	5.75	3.13	2.04	71.02	3.68	13.48	2.16
	4390	6.00	3.20	2.74	72.23	3.75	12.08	1.93
	4391	5.95	2.65	2.68	71.34	4.25	13.13	2.10
Montana	4196	7.55	1.70	2.60	74.53	3.99	9.03	1.54
	4197	6.60	3.00	2.52	74.20	3.35	10.33	1.65
	4415	4.95	3.15	2.58	76.79	3.10	9.45	1.51
South Carolina	4299	6.83	2.65	2.45	73.62	4.10	10.33	1.65
Kentucky	4122	6.00	2.90	2.37	75.73	4.25	8.75	1.40
Utah	4319	7.70	3.40	2.53	72.99	2.88	10.50	1.68
Arizona	4164	6.26	2.90	2.63	74.30	4.28	9.63	1.54
Washington	4435	5.95	3.50	2.98	70.97	4.35	12.25	1.96
Oregon	4275	6.27	3.05	2.06	72.89	3.83	11.90	1.90
	4277	0.20	2.78	2.71	75.56	4.00	8.75	1.40
California	4016	6.70	2.74	3.01	74.32	4.14	9.10	1.46
	4374	4.53	4.43	2.72	74.74	4.48	9.10	1.46
	4378	6.18	2.74	2.50	75.52	4.13	8.93	1.43
Wyoming	4423	6.70	2.20	2.52	74.03	3.00	11.55	1.85
Colorado	3584	8.15	2.77	2.87	68.99	3.92	13.30	2.13

Average composition of American barleys (unhulled), arranged by States.

State.	Number of analyses.	Water.	Ash.	Oil.	Carbhy-drates.	Fiber.	Albuminoids.	Nitrogen.
		Per ct.	Per ct.	Per ct.	Per ct.	Per ct.	Per ct.	Per ct.
United States	90	6.53	2.89	2.68	72.77	3.80	11.33	1.81
Atlantic Slope	10	6.64	2.51	2.50	73.02	3.57	11.59	1.85
Northern States	48	6.55	2.87	2.69	72.53	3.76	11.58	1.85
Western States	30	6.66	2.96	2.73	72.20	3.87	11.52	1.84
Northwestern States	8	6.02	2.85	2.69	73.03	3.59	11.82	....
Pacific Slope	10	6.47	3.05	2.65	72.43	3.90	11.50	1.69
Vermont	3	6.56	2.51	2.77	71.41	3.84	12.89	2.06
Connecticut	1	6.50	2.90	2.34	75.14	2.89	10.15	1.62
New York	5	6.77	2.46	2.65	73.59	3.50	11.03	1.76
Pennsylvania	1	6.27	3.05	2.06	72.89	3.83	11.90	1.90
Ohio	4	6.68	3.25	2.64	72.95	4.19	10.28	1.64
Michigan	5	6.27	2.79	2.72	72.34	3.42	12.46	1.99
Indiana	2	5.95	3.23	3.13	73.28	3.99	10.42	1.67
Illinois	4	6.37	3.08	2.67	71.84	3.66	12.38	1.98
Wisconsin	5	7.05	2.95	2.63	71.87	4.05	11.45	1.83
Minnesota	5	7.29	2.63	2.81	72.87	4.01	10.39	1.66
Iowa	4	6.27	3.08	2.71	71.37	4.01	12.56	2.01
Nebraska	1	7.58	3.00	2.70	71.12	3.35	12.25	1.98
Dakota	5	5.81	2.99	2.77	71.75	3.66	13.02	2.08
Montana	3	6.37	2.62	2.56	75.17	3.48	9.80	1.57
South Carolina	1	6.85	2.63	2.45	73.02	4.10	10.33	1.65
Kentucky	1	6.00	2.90	2.37	75.73	4.25	8.75	1.40
Utah	1	7.70	3.40	2.53	72.99	2.88	10.50	1.68
Arizona	1	6.26	2.90	2.03	74.30	4.28	9.63	1.54
Washington	1	5.95	3.50	2.98	70.97	4.35	12.25	1.96
Oregon	2	6.23	2.92	2.38	74.23	3.01	10.33	1.65
California	3	5.80	3.30	2.74	74.86	4.25	9.05	1.45
Wyoming	1	6.70	2.20	2.52	74.03	3.00	11.55	1.85
Colorado	1	8.15	2.77	2.87	68.99	3.02	13.30	2.13

DISCUSSION OF THE DATA AND AVERAGES.

As Canadian barley forms the greater portion of our supply, it will be considered first, and that of the United States compared with it.

Maercker found that the finest grain contained not more than 8 per cent. of albuminoids and consisted of at least 80 per cent. of mealy kernels. These two factors, together with the brightness of the grain, he considered to be the characteristics by which its quality should be judged.

Of the twelve typical specimens of last year's Canadian crop none were below 9 per cent. of albuminoids, the average being 9.83, and only six contained 60 per cent. of kernels which were mealy or half mealy in structure. They cannot be said therefore to be equal to what are considered extremely fine barley in Germany. They do, however, reach and in most cases exceed the average production of foreign countries, and may be considered as of extremely good quality for samples from actual trade lots, and better than those produced the world over, as may be seen by comparison with the investigations which have been quoted on previous pages. In weight per bushel they are about the same as the average of Maercker, and in moisture, as with all our grain, much drier than the product of damper climates.

The differences in the different grades are marked almost entirely by brightness and perfection of the kernel, there being a remarkably clos agreement in all other respects. This shows how important a factor climate and care in harvesting and handling are in enhancing or depreciating the value of the grain. The latter factor, care, is almost entirely within the control of the farmer, while varying seasons, of course, influence the former. Of the different districts that north of Lake Erie produces the specimens richest in nitrogen, which would therefore be graded lowest as far as this influences our judgment, thus agreeing with current opinion. In mealiness these specimens are much ahead of all the others, and this ought to more than balance the slightly higher percentage of albuminoids. The summer rains, however, by coloring the grain have the greatest influence in determining quality, and eventually make the barley of this district the least desirable. The remaining districts, north of Ontario, produce grain much alike, that from the B district averaging heavier in weight per bushel, and that from D being a little less nitrogenous. As a whole these Canadian barleys certainly form a very good standard of reference.

BARLEYS OF THE UNITED STATES.

In comparing the barleys of the United States with those of Canada, it appears at once that, as a whole, the former average about as mealy in consistency as the latter. Examined by distribution geographically, the Eastern grain is found to be much less mealy than the Western, that of the Northwest being the richest in mealy kernels. Again, however, we find that but two out of sixty-four samples contained 80 per cent. or over of mealy or half-mealy kernels. In weight per bushel there is no variation from Canadian and foreign grain, but in size the barleys of the United States, as a whole, are larger than those of Canada. Unfortunately we have no data for those of foreign production. The Eastern grain is no larger than the Canadian, and the average is increased by the large size of that from the Northwest and the Pacific Slope, which at the same time has an increased weight per bushel.

In brightness, the samples from those portions of the country having a dry climate at harvest time, especially the Pacific Slope and the Northwest, were far superior. This is an important feature in considering the best areas for the production of good malting barley; and while California as yet furnishes almost nothing for brewing purposes, it would seem to be one of our best fields. The high percentage of albuminoids stored up in the peculiar climate of the Northwest, while an advantage in the wheat grain, would be a serious objection in barley. In this respect it appears that the average amount of albuminoids in the barley of the United States is greater than that of Canada, and far ahead of anything which Maercker would consider desirable. California alone is 1 per cent. below the average for the rest of the country, there being less than one-half per cent. difference from 11.50 per cent. in the average for all but California, which has 10.50 per cent. This is higher than was found in the Canadian grain, so that it may safely be said that the latter is at present the best in the market and superior to our own.

Among the analyses the following extremes are found:

	Highest.	State.	Lowest.	State.
	Per cent.		Per cent.	
Water	9.15	Minnesota..	4.53	California.
Ash	4.43	California..	1.50	Minnesota.
Oil	3.54	Indiana.....	2.06	Oregon.
Carbhydrates	76.79	Montana ...	68.99	Colorado.
Crude fiber	4.05	Ohio	2.64	Illinois.
Albuminoids	14.88	Dakota	8.75	Kentucky and Oregon.
Weight of 100 grains ....drams..	4.900	California..	2.630	Pennsylvania.
Weight per bushel ....pounds..	60.2	Utah	50.4	Do.
Per ct. of mealy and half mealy kernels....	100.00	Montana....	16.0	Vermont.

Dakota sustains its reputation for high nitrogen and Oregon for low, but the variations in this constituent are not as wide as in wheat, barley, like rye, appearing to be less affected in this respect, although Maercker's experiments show that barley responds in its percentage of albuminoids readily to nitrogenous manuring. His seed was, however, very poor in albuminoids—7.7–8.0 per cent.—and would naturally increase when the conditions were made favorable.

In Koenig's collection of analyses of this grain he gives as the average of 127 specimens:

	Per cent.
Water	13.77
Ash	2.69
Oil	2.16
Carbhydrates	64.93
Crude fiber	5.31
Albuminoids	11.14
Total	100.00

This is but little different from the average production of the United States, and would point to the fact that our country, at any rate in certain portions, produces as good malting barley as others. Canada is a witness to this fact, as shown by the specimens which have been examined from there, which are well above foreign averages in starchiness. Experience and care have taught the Canadians, in connection with their favorable climate, the means of producing an excellent grain, superior to other parts of the country. It seems quite possible for the farmers in many portions of the United States, and especially California, the climatic conditions of which are such as to avoid damaging summer rains, with no too dry and hot a climate, to increase our supply of barley of good quality by attention to the conditions which have been mentioned, and thus prevent the necessity of importing grain which should be produced at home.

There is one condition which in the case of wheat was found to be of evident effect. Although almost all the specimens examined were spring-sown grain, twelve of winter barley were found to contain but 10.05 per cent. of albuminoid, as compared to 11.42 in the spring varieties. Whether this could be made of any importance in practice cannot of course be decided except by the possibilities of the culture of winter barleys, which as yet seem to be small. Our dry and hot climate, ripening the grain before it has had time to fill out the kernel with starch, and the liability to discoloration from summer showers, are the two disadvantages we have to contend with.

In a few samples the hull or husk was detached from the grain and the amount determined.

Barley—percentage of grain and hulls.

Number.	Grain.	Hull.	Number.	Grain.	Hull.
	Per cent.	Per cent.		Per cent.	Per cent.
4015	83.06	16.94	4179	86.28	13.72
4081	83.78	16.22	4202	84.93	15.07
4090	83.70	16.30	4205	87.45	12.55
4097	84.25	15.75	4220	84.96	15.04
4107	85.72	14.28			
4156	84.01	15.99	Average	84.78	15.22
4166	84.47	15.53			

The extreme amounts are 16.94 and 12.55 per cent; not nearly as large as is the case with oats.

The composition of these specimens was as follows:

Composition of American barleys (hulled), arranged by States.

State.	Serial number.	Water.	Ash.	Oil.	Carbhydrates.	Fiber.	Albuminoids.	Nitrogen.
		Per cent.	Per cent.	Per cent.	Per cent.	Per cent.	Per cent.	Per cent.
New York	4220	6.88	1.88	2.20	75.22	1.22	12.60	2.02
Do	4235	6.25	2.40	2.60	76.27	1.98	10.50	1.88
Michigan	4156	5.55	2.35	2.84	76.14	1.74	11.38	1.82
Indiana	4081	0.55	2.20	2.30	73.77	1.88	13.30	2.13
Minnesota	4166	5.60	2.20	2.55	76.91	1.19	11.55	1.85
Do	4179	6.00	2.10	2.76	76.35	1.41	11.38	1.82
Iowa	4090	6.41	2.15	3.12	74.67	2.27	11.38	1.82
Do	4097	6.35	1.98	2.65	75.52	1.25	12.25	1.96
Do	4107	6.25	2.15	2.76	75.19	1.40	12.25	1.96
Missouri	4188	7.50	2.02	2.81	73.95	1.47	12.25	1.96
Nevada	4202	7.20	2.38	2.77	75.93	1.92	9.80	1.57
Do	4205	2.87	1.99	2.47	81.31	1.73	9.63	1.54
California	4015	5.80	2.60	2.61	76.03	1.23	11.73	1.88
Do	4382	6.85	2.05	2.61	74.49	1.40	12.00	2.02
Colorado	3584	7.78	2.30	2.86	71.10	1.90	14.00	2.24

Average composition of American barleys (hulled), arranged by States.

State.	No. of analyses.	Water.	Ash.	Oil.	Carbhydrates.	Fiber.	Albuminoids.	Nitrogen.
		Per cent.	Per cent.	Per cent.	Per cent.	Per cent.	Per cent.	
United States	15	6.26	2.18	2.66	75.53	1.60	11.77	1.88
Northern States	10	6.34	2.14	2.66	75.40	1.58	11.88	1.90
Western States	5	6.10	2.27	2.66	75.78	1.64	11.55	1.75
New York	2	6.57	2.14	2.40	75.74	1.60	11.55	1.85
Michigan	1	5.55	2.35	2.84	76.14	1.44	11.38	1.82
Indiana	1	6.55	2.20	2.30	73.77	1.88	13.30	2.13
Minnesota	2	5.80	2.15	2.66	76.63	1.30	11.46	1.83
Iowa	3	6.34	2.09	2.84	75.13	1.64	11.96	1.91
Missouri	1	7.50	2.02	2.81	73.95	1.47	12.25	1.96
Nevada	2	5.04	2.28	2.62	78.02	1.83	0.71	1.55
California	2	6.33	2.32	2.61	75.26	1.32	12.16	1.95
Colorado	1	7.78	2.30	2.86	71.16	1.90	14.00	2.24

The changes are merely such as one would expect from the removal of the fibrous hull. The percentages of albuminoids, fiber, and carbhydrates are increased, that of ash and water diminished. The results are merely of value to serve as a comparison of this cereal in its hull-less condition with the other cereals in a similar state.

Our investigations as a whole seem to prove that, while at present Canadian barleys are superior to those grown in the United States, the result is due more to a lack of understanding of the proper localities and methods of cultivation than in any obstacle in the way of extending the production to an extent to do away with our dependence on importation. Field experiments are now most desirable as a means of deciding upon the best varieties and methods as soon as a study of the climatic conditions shall enable us to select those portions of the country best suited to this cereal. In time, no doubt, California, whose climate in many parts is well adapted to the growth of barley for malting purposes, will make itself felt if, as appears probable, the quality of her barleys in the market answers to the expectations raised by laboratory examination.

ANALYSES OF OATS, BARLEY, AND RYE IN DETAIL.

In our first report several analyses of wheat were published in which the carbhydrates were separated into their proportions of sugars, starch, and gum, and the albuminoids into those soluble in alcohol of 80 per cent. strength and those insoluble. In the Annual Report of the Department for 1878 several analyses of corn were presented in the same way. For comparison with these results, which are of interest, several have been made of oats, barley, and rye:

Analyses of oats, barley, and rye in detail.

OATS.

Number.	Weight of 100 grains.	Moisture.	Ash.	Fat.	Sugar, &c.	Dextrine, &c.	Starch.	Albuminoids soluble in 80 per cent. alcohol.	Albuminoids insoluble in 80 per cent. alcohol.	Fiber.	Total nitrogen.	Total nitrogen × 6.25.
3044	2.090	6.32	2.25	7.86	5.59	3.68	58.87	.97	13.56	.90	2.32	14.58
3045	1.756	5.93	2.38	8.25	6.21	3.08	59.04	1.09	11.26	1.56	2.07	12.95
3049 (4)	1.798	6.57	2.02	8.64	5.84	3.12	58.34	1.50	12.68	1.29	2.27	14.18
3078	1.878	8.00	2.17	4.48	6.02	3.96	58.29	1.72	14.21	1.15	2.55	15.93
3008	1.084	7.38	2.61	7.60	5.96	.40	60.81	1.86	12.32	1.08	2.27	14.18
3127	1.892	6.08	3.07	7.83	5.67	2.82	60.18	2.15	11.15	1.05	2.13	13.30
3175	1.495	7.07	2.38	7.23	5.67	3.90	58.47	1.95	11.88	1.45	2.21	13.83
3187	1.922	7.21	1.95	8.15	5.06	3.56	58.24	1.36	12.64	1.23	2.24	14.00
3210	1.780	6.95	2.45	8.21	6.56	4.52	53.56	2.43	14.02	1.30	2.63	16.45
3235	2.139	7.28	1.78	8.52	5.80	3.86	58.08	2.20	11.28	1.20	2.16	13.48
3243	1.703	6.34	2.08	6.98	6.28	3.82	54.02	1.42	16.02	1.60	2.88	18.04
3260	1.048	6.99	2.43	7.75	6.39	3.78	56.17	2.71	12.55	1.23	2.44	15.26
3262	1.606	6.78	2.07	7.40	6.10	3.42	53.69	2.78	16.06	1.10	3.11	19.44
3270	1.656	6.77	2.20	8.88	6.52	3.60	56.25	(?)	14.53	1.25	2.32	14.53
3323	1.506	7.00	2.06	8.12	5.43	3.42	54.31	1.15	17.05	1.46	2.91	18.20
3335	1.595	6.13	2.35	8.58	6.43	3.48	56.04	2.31	12.57	1.51	2.38	14.88
3301	1.313	8.75	2.15	9.47	6.50	3.86	56.08	2.70	9.20	1.29	1.90	11.90
3411	1.355	6.05	1.60	7.77	6.69	3.58	52.59	1.83	17.42	1.57	3.08	19.25

BARLEY.

Number.	Weight of 100 grains.	Moisture.	Ash.	Fat.	Sugar, &c.	Dextrine, &c.	Starch.	Albuminoids soluble in 80 per cent. alcohol.	Albuminoids insoluble in 80 per cent. alcohol.	Fiber.	Total nitrogen.	Total nitrogen × 6.25.
4067	2.920	6.52	3.08	2.66	7.71	3.60	60.46	4.25	8.35	3.37	2.02	12.60
4098	3.010	5.69	3.18	2.75	5.82	3.48	62.98	3.18	8.55	4.37	1.88	11.73
4151	3.450	6.44	2.97	2.70	7.12	3.92	60.29	3.76	9.37	3.43	2.10	13.13
4153	2.280	6.37	2.59	2.73	8.73	4.04	56.36	4.79	9.91	3.88	2.35	14.70
4169	2.610	7.60	1.50	2.69	5.97	3.58	61.24	2.85	8.00	3.57	1.74	10.85
4198	2.830	7.58	3.00	2.80	8.30		62.72	4.38	7.87	3.35	1.96	12.25
4233	3.380	6.95	2.64	2.66	6.01	3.14	65.32	3.07	7.08	3.13	1.62	10.15
4243	3.410	7.39	2.45	2.48	6.93	3.80	62.37	3.41	7.44	3.73	1.71	10.65
4209	3.170	6.25	3.07	2.40	6.21	3.40	63.52	3.01	7.49	4.65	1.68	10.50
4277	5.110	6.20	2.78	2.71	5.38	3.46	66.72	2.86	5.89	4.00	1.40	8.75
4324	3.480	6.50	2.40	2.65	7.79	3.00	61.58	4.23	8.37	3.48	2.02	12.60
4326	2.980	6.55	2.90	2.75	7.60	3.40	60.57	4.02	8.06	4.15	1.93	12.08
4374	4.550	4.53	4.43	2.72	7.44	3.42	63.88	3.42	5.68	4.48	1.46	9.10
4300	2.710	6.00	3.20	2.74	7.21	3.76	61.32	3.95	8.13	3.75	1.93	12.08

RYE.

Number.	Weight of 100 grains.	Moisture.	Ash.	Fat.	Sugar, &c.	Dextrine, &c.	Starch.	Albuminoids soluble in 80 per cent. alcohol.	Albuminoids insoluble in 80 per cent. alcohol.	Fiber.	Total nitrogen.	Total nitrogen × 6.25.
5029	2.516	9.69	1.88	1.80	8.10	4.76	62.52	2.20	7.60	1.45	1.57	9.80
5052	1.240	8.24	1.91	2.17	7.93	4.50	60.47	3.17	9.78	1.83	2.07	12.95
5075	1.840	8.45	2.36	1.98	8.49	4.38	59.61	3.45	9.68	1.00	2.10	13.13
5079	1.670	9.18	1.02	1.70	6.25	4.56	64.34	2.17	9.03	1.15	1.79	11.20
5107	2.034	8.32	2.08	1.03	6.02	4.54	63.55	2.14	9.24	1.28	1.82	11.38
5116	2.250	8.85	2.06	1.93	7.81	5.54	60.35	3.11	8.07	1.38	1.93	12.08
5140	2.164	9.70	2.10	1.91	7.29	5.32	60.55	2.44	9.26	1.38	1.88	11.73
5215	2.670	8.03	2.03	1.74	6.20	6.02	62.12	1.76	9.97	1.23	1.88	11.73
5231	2.310	8.98	2.16	1.69	7.85	5.19	61.33	2.17	9.38	1.25	1.85	11.55
5248	1.873	8.75	2.01	1.85	7.52	4.20	62.74	2.18	9.20	1.55	1.82	11.38
5269	2.080	8.15	1.70	1.93	7.80	4.14	62.23	2.71	9.37	1.88	1.93	12.08
5282	2.422	9.35	2.15	1.86	9.46	4.44	59.81	3.08	8.65	1.20	1.88	11.73
5290	2.154	9.75	2.10	1.70	6.74	4.36	63.31	1.90	8.25	1.89	1.62	10.15
5348	2.064	8.35	2.69	1.75	7.89	4.44	58.73	3.03	9.05	1.54	1.93	12.08
5351	2.012	8.65	2.32	1.80	7.10	5.00	62.40	2.70	8.44	1.77	1.79	11.20
5357	1.087	8.80	1.96	1.84	7.45	4.46	62.50	2.56	8.99	1.35	1.85	11.55
5360	1.846	8.38	1.90	1.38	7.83	4.80	62.19	2.15	9.39	1.56	1.90	11.90

The sources of the specimens will be found under their respective serial numbers in the general descriptive tables. They are from various parts of the country, and represent fairly the average production and variations.

For comparison, averages of the above results have been drawn, as well as of those of wheat and corn previously published, excluding the Colorado wheats.

Averages of detailed analyses of cereals.

	Wheat.	Corn.	Oats.	Barley.	Rye.
No. of analyses	27	21	18	14	17
Water	9.25	9.34	6.92	6.47	8.85
Ash	1.84	1.54	2.22	2.87	2.0d
Oil	2.30	5.54	7.87	2.67	1.83
Sugar, &c	3.50	2.18	6.07	7.02	7.57
Dextrine and sal starch	2.30	2.18	3.47	3.55	4.75
Starch	67.88	66.91	56.91	62.09	61.87
Albuminoids soluble in 80 per cent. alcohol	3.58	5.84	1.82	3.66	2.53
Albuminoids insoluble in 80 per cent. alcohol	7.45	4.96	13.43	7.86	9.07
Fiber	1.90	1.41	1.29	3.81	1.47
	100.00	100.00	100.00	100.00	100.00
Total albuminoids	11.03	10.80	14.25	11.52	11.60

From the figures it is seen that oats and barley are much drier than the remaining cereals. This is due in the case of both to the outer chaffy covering, which readily gives up its water. In the oats, however, this had been removed, but its effect in abstracting moisture has evidently remained. The smaller size of the rye kernel, no doubt, accounts for its somewhat lower moisture than wheat and corn, and this, too, has perhaps an effect upon oats.

Of all the grains barley is the richest in ash—this, too, probably due to its hull—followed by oats, the richest actually in ash in kernel.

In oil, oats is ahead of corn by over 2 per cent., and far ahead of all the other cereals.

In sugar, barley and rye are superior, with oats comparatively rich, and corn the poorest.

In dextrine or gum, rye is the richest, having twice as much as wheat and corn, and 1 per cent. more than oats and barley.

The accumulation of its many other constituents makes oats by far the least starchy of the cereals, followed by rye and barley, with wheat as the most starchy. This latter fact, from a flouring point of view, is important, taken in connection with the character of the nitrogen of wheat and its small amount of oil. Of the determinations of the nitrogenous constituents it must be said that the solubility does not show much in regard to their quality. Part of the gluten of wheat goes into the alcohol extract and part remains insoluble, the latter being chiefly the gluten-casien. In corn the soluble portion is known often as zein and is more distinctive than the soluble albuminoids of the other cereals.

It is the largest in amount of the soluble nitrogenous constituents found in any of the grains, exceeding the insoluble portion. Oats, on the other hand, contains the least soluble albumen.

Barley is, in the condition in which it was analyzed, most fibrous, but in its hulless state no more so than wheat. Aside from this the most fiber is found in wheat and the least in oats. From the averages wide variations will be found among individual analyses, which are due to circumstances of environment which our data do not at present permit a study of. A large increase of analyses and conditions which may in time accumulate will render this possible.

MILLING PRODUCTS.

In our second report an examination of the products of roller milling was presented, with especial reference to the process as applied to the hard spring wheats of the Northwest. This examination has since been extended to the winter wheats of Kansas, as represented by the products of a small roller mill at Ottawa. The data are as follows:

Mill products from Ottawa, Kans.

Description of sample.	Serial number.	Water.	Ash.	Oil.	Carbohydrates.	Fiber.	Albumen.	Nitrogen.	Moist. gluten.
		Pr. ct.	Pr. ct.	Pr. ct.	Pr. ct.	Pr. ct.	Pr. ct.	Pr. ct.	Pr. ct.
Whole wheat	6014	9.55	1.78	1.27	72.97	1.88	12.25	1.96	30.72
First break	6015	8.68	1.90	2.22	72.67	1.93	12.60	2.02	31.74
Second break	6016	9.15	1.85	2.17	71.57	2.48	12.78	2.04	27.18
Third break	6017	9.30	2.13	2.16	71.19	2.26	12.96	2.07	27.63
Fourth break	6018	8.18	2.55	2.62	70.63	2.77	13.65	2.18	24.90
Fifth break	6019	9.40	4.15	3.41	63.81	4.00	15.23	2.44	
Sixth break	6020	7.60	5.20	3.99	62.56	5.60	15.05	2.41	
Bran	6021	8.45	6.30	4.64	58.28	6.60	15.75	2.52	
Ship-stuff or shorts	6022	8.18	3.38	5.05	62.45	2.84	17.50	2.80	
Chop	6023	11.40	.78	2.00	73.56	1.23	11.03	1.70	26.14
Fine middlings	6024	11.43	.38	1.11	75.28	.42	11.36	1.82	29.10
Medium middlings	6025	11.03	.50	1.29	74.93	1.40	10.85	1.74	28.76
Coarse middlings	6026	8.88	.83	1.84	77.25	.70	10.50	1.68	29.09 / 20.13
Germ middlings	6027	10.75	2.30	3.99	67.09	1.69	14.18	2.27	
Tailings from fine middlings purified	6028	9.60	3.10	5.07	63.22	1.86	17.15	3.74	
Finished germ	6029	8.70	5.20	7.47	54.91	3.59	20.13	3.22	
Reduction of tailings from third middlings	6030	11.35	.43	1.23	75.39	.40	11.20	1.79	28.45
Fine middling flour	6031	11.25	.33	6.05	71.06	.46	10.85	1.74	25.02
Second grade flour	6032	11.30	.38	1.15	75.91	.40	10.85	1.74	27.75
Flour from coarse middlings	6033	10.85	.30	.93	78.60	.12	9.20	1.48	23.79
Flour from first break	6034	11.50	.68	.96	78.13	.85	7.88	1.26	19.28
Break flour from second, third, fourth, and fifth break	6035	11.42	.43	1.06	76.89	.22	9.98	1.60	27.53
Straight-grade flour	6036	11.90	.35	1.01	76.34	.25	10.15	1.52	25.65
Patent flour	6037	11.02	.35	1.01	77.80	.19	9.63	1.54	22.07
Low-grade flour	6038	10.60	.85	2.00	72.29	.52	13.65	2.18	41.67
Flour from third middlings	6039	12.48	.32	1.17	73.75	.20	12.08	1.93	33.83

The winter wheat from which the Kansas products were obtained is a larger and softer grain than the spring varieties of Minnesota. It is much less oily than the usual production of the country at large, and while above the average in nitrogenous constituents and representing about the usual percentage found in that portion of the country where it was grown, it is of course lower in albuminoids than the Minnesota grain. The relative results in the breaks are, however, about the same in both cases. There is a somewhat greater accumulation of ash and fiber in the last breaks, and the shorts are proportionately richer in nitrogen. This is hardly what would be expected in milling softer wheats, but shows that the process is as effective as with spring varieties in separating the endosperm or floury portion of the grain from the outer coats. The increase in the ash and fiber may be due, however, to a larger proportion of germ in the branny products than is the case in Minnesota.

The grading and purification of the middlings in the two mills is so different that it is difficult to make a comparison of their relative purity. The finest middlings are in both cases the most impure, carrying the most bran and germ, and consequently being rich in nitrogen. The tailings from the purification of these middlings are largely germ and bran, and are very rich in ash, oil, and albuminoids. The flour from the fine middlings is richer in both cases in nitrogen, owing to its contamination with germ and bran, and the best is produced from the coarse. There is a somewhat less relative proportion of the total albuminoids of the wheat in the coarse middlings flour of winter than of spring wheat, a condition which is also observed in the finished products, patent and straight grades. The low grade of the Kansas mill will be seen to be quite different from that so called in Minnesota. It is, it seems, more nearly what is there known as a baker's grade. The low grade from spring wheat, while rich in nitrogen from the amount of bran and germ it contains, is very poor in gluten. The baker's grade from that grain is not only rich in nitrogen but also in gluten; with this the low-grade Kansas flour corresponds, due probably to the fact that in the smaller mill the process of refinement is not carried to such extremes. In the finished germ there is also visible a vast difference. It is not separated in as clean and entire condition from the winter wheat, either owing to lack of facilities or difficulties in the way, and is consequently less rich in nitrogen. The break flours present, too, as great a contrast as the low grade, that from Kansas being much more starchy and less glutinous or stiff. It is of better quality, for, although poor in gluten, it does not containing as much germ.

Depending largely on the original wheat, the finished products in Kansas are not as stiff as those from spring grain, but this was to be expected, and the greatest differences which have been observed are due fully as much, as far as we can judge, to method of manufacture as to physical differences in the grain. That there are some to be ascribed to this cause is evident from the lower relation of the purer products in Kansas to the original grain. This was observed also in roller flours from Ohio and Washington, D. C., in our former investigations.

There seems to be every advantage over ordinary milling with stones in the use of this process with our winter wheats, both in economy and quality, although, perhaps, not as great as with the hard Northwestern.

grain, nor as large in small as in large mills. The rapid extension of the system shows that practice has demonstrated what chemical and physical investigations have shown to be advisable, and it seems from a comparison of our analyses of the two series that the more the products are differentiated the more satisfactory are the results.

In another place an investigation of the proximate composition of the germ will soon be published, showing the presence of remarkably large amounts of cane sugar, together with another sugar not yet identified, and proving not to be raffinose; and of allantoin, a nitrogenous substance hitherto found only once as a plant constituent and whose presence is of great importance from a botanico-physiological point of view.

MISCELLANEOUS ANALYSES OF CEREALS.

In the routine work of the division many miscellaneous samples of cereals have been from time to time examined. The results are here collected. The sources from which they have been derived are as follows:

Sources of specimens.

WHEAT.

2763. From New Zealand. Selected sample. Crop of 1884.
2764. From Mr. McLaughlin, New Jerusalem, Ventura County, California. Crop of 1884.
2765. From Charles Woodhull, Wahpeton, Dak. Crop of 1884.

CORN.

1978. Bessarabian. From S. M. Clark, Washington, D. C. Crop of 1884.
2438. From T. J. Higgins, Morris County, Kansas. A fine large-eared Yellow Dent.
2428. From S. M. Clark, Washington, D. C. Crop raised from seed 2438. This sample the less perfect and most shriveled kernels of one cob. Crop of 1884.
2429. From S. M. Clark, Washington, D. C. The perfect and plump kernels of the above-mentioned cob.
2430. From Lake County, Tennessee. 1883. White Dent.
2431. From Giles County, Tennessee. 1883. White Dent.
2432. From Bradley County, Tennessee. 1883. White Dent.
2433. From Clay County, Kentucky. 1883. White Dent.
2434. From Brown County, Minnesota. 1883. White Dent.
2435. From Herkimer County, New York. 1883. Yellow Flint.
2436. From Jackson County, Minnesota. 1883. Red Dent.
2437. From Watonwan County, Minnesota. 1883. Yellow Dent.
2440. From ———, Florida. 1884. Yellow Dent.

OATS.

1973-5. From the collection of the Atchison, Topeka and Santa Fé Railroad. Grown in Kansas.
1976. From J. P. Hooke, Marysville, Tenn. Winter variety.
1977. From R. B. Potter, M. D., Dade County, Florida.
2766. Distributed by the Department. 1885. Welcome Oats.
2766. Distributed by the Department. 1885. Clydedale Oats.
3000. From New Zealand. 40 pounds per bushel. Crop of 1884.

RYE.

1971-2. From the collection of the Atchison, Topeka and Santa Fé Railroad. Grown in Kansas.

BARLEY.

1978. Distributed by the Department. 1884. Imperial.

The analyses are as follows:

Miscellaneous analyses, 1884-'85.

Cereals.	Serial number.	Locality.	Weight of 100 grains.	Water.	Ash.	Oil.	Carbhy-drates.	Crude fiber.	Albumi-noids.	Nitrogen.
Wheat	2763	New Zealand	5.036	9.40	1.25	1.76	71.49	1.75	14.35	2.30
	2764	California		7.00	2.45	4.95	71.32	2.90	11.38	1.82
	2765	Dakota		8.55	1.85	3.01	71.51	1.95	13.13	2.10
Corn (maize) kernel	1978	Dist. of Columbia		8.70	1.75	4.44	72.67	1.24	11.20	1.79
	2428	Dist. of Columbia		10.75	1.45	3.48	75.52	1.80	7.00	1.12
	2429	Dist. of Columbia		10.12	1.35	4.32	75.51	1.70	7.00	1.12
	2438	Kansas		10.00	1.50	4.37	71.38	1.90	10.85	1.74
	2430	Tennessee		11.15	2.05	4.34	72.18	1.70	8.58	1.37
	2431	Tennessee		9.65	2.05	4.95	71.32	2.40	9.63	1.54
	2432	Tennessee		10.45	1.65	4.57	71.73	2.15	9.45	1.51
	2433	Kentucky		10.55	1.70	4.17	73.10	1.90	8.58	1.37
	2434	Minnesota		9.60	1.75	4.53	72.55	2.12	9.45	1.51
	2435	New York		8.50	1.45	4.51	71.62	2.02	11.90	1.90
	2436	Minnesota		9.80	2.00	4.01	71.76	2.10	10.33	1.65
	2437	Minnesota		10.50	1.65	4.05	71.40	2.07	10.33	1.65
	2440	Florida		8.47	1.37	4.82	72.99	2.02	10.33	1.65
Oats	1973	Kansas		8.76	2.55	7.15	65.96		15.58	2.49
	1974	Kansas		8.87	2.60	5.79	68.39		14.35	2.32
	1975	Kansas		8.37	2.75	8.14	64.11		16.63	2.66
	1976	Tennessee		9.05	2.09	9.42	63.71		15.75	2.52
	1977	Florida		9.07	2.45	9.43	65.22		13.83	2.21
	2766	Imported		9.60	2.40	8.83	64.82		14.35	2.30
	2767	Imported				9.02				
	3000	New Zealand		*10.18	*2.32	*8.91	*65.34	*1.70	*11.55	*1.85
	3000	New Zealand		†7.60	†5.50	†.80	63.44	†20.56	*2.10	†.34
Rye	1971	Kansas		11.60	1.60	2.22	70.49	1.49	12.60	2.02
	1972	Kansas		11.20	1.80	1.84	71.32	1.40	12.40	1.99
Barley	1984	?		8.46	2.45	2.71	73.01	1.82	11.55	1.85

* Kernel 70.6 per cent.   † Hulls 29.45 per cent.

It is unnecessary to call particular attention to these analyses. The New Zealand wheat was a selected exhibition sample, very large and heavy, and of rather a soft character. It is rather poor in ash and oil, and quite rich in albuminoids.

The specimens from California and Dakota sustain the usual reputation of the grain from those States.

The samples of corn vary very little in composition for the different localities. The only exception which it is of interest to observe is in the case of the plump and shriveled grains grown in the District of Columbia from seed produced in Kansas. While not varying at all among themselves in composition, the plump and shriveled grains have departed quite remarkably from the composition of the parent seed from Kansas. Among the remaining specimens the usual narrow limits of variation in this cereal are seen. Even Minnesota, which produces a wheat rich in nitrogen, does not excel in its corn in this respect.

The analyses of oats show no peculiarities; the sample from New

Zealand alone is rather low in albuminoids and not corresponding to the wheat with which it was associated. The kernels were analyzed free from hulls.

ANALYSIS OF WHEATS OF THE CROP OF 1885.

Recently several Minnesota wheats, harvested during the season of 1885, have been examined. They sustain the averages of previous years, or are slightly richer in albuminoids. The results follows together with those of seed wheats distributed by the Department in the autumn of 1885, the products of which it is hoped may be compared another year.

Analysis of wheats from Minnesota, 1885.

Variety.	Serial No.	Weight of 100 grains.	Water.	Ash.	Oil.	Carbhydrates.	Crude fiber.	Albuminoids.	Nitrogen.	Moist gluten.
		Grains.	Per c.	Per c.	Per c.	Per c.	Per c.	Per c.	Per c.	Per c.
Rice	6000	4.114	9.40	2.08	2.79	70.33	1.92	13.48	2.16	29.37
Blue Stem	6001	3.096	9.13	2.03	2.94	69.48	2.42	14.00	2.14	29.41
Scotch Fife	6002	2.649	9.18	2.43	2.65	70.47	1.79	13.48	2.10	32.31
Scotch Fife	6003	2.190	9.38	1.70	2.98	69.06	1.83	15.05	2.41	32.07
Scotch Fife	6004	2.565	8.93	2.03	2.89	68.75	2.00	15.40	2.46	38.45

Analysis of winter wheats distributed by the Department, November, 1885.

Variety.	Serial No.	Weight of 100 grains.	Weight per bushel.	Water.	Ash.	Oil.	Carbhydrates.	Crude fiber.	Albuminoids.	Nitrogen.	Moist gluten.
		Grains.	Lbs.	Per c.	Per c.	Per c.	Per c.	Per c.	Per c.	Per c.	Per c.
Four-Rowed Sheriff	6005	3.734	65.8	10.28	1.95	2.29	73.52	1.81	10.15	1.62	26.54
Red Mediterranean	6006	4.635	67.2	11.05	1.63	2.22	71.25	1.60	12.25	1.96	31.66
Diehl-Mediterranean	6007	4.222	65.8	10.45	1.65	2.25	72.97	2.00	10.68	1.72	32.22
Indian Winter	6008	3.126	65.5	10.2J	2.23	2.06	72.24	1.72	11.55	1.85	19.16
White Crimean	6009	6.086	66.5	10.73	2.00	2.55	70.63	1.66	12.43	1.99	00.00
McGehee White	6010	2.990	66.4	10.48	1.88	2.22	71.34	1.83	12.25	1.96	33.61
Extra Early Oakley	6011	3.945	66.3	11.45	1.20	2.29	68.79	1.79	13.48	2.16	32.95
Genoese	6012	4.113	68.7	9.68	1.73	2.04	74.68	1.89	9.98	1.60	22.61
Egyptian	6013	5.308	68.6	9.83	1.78	2.04	74.52	1.50	10.33	1.65	29.43
	6040	(?)	(?)	9.88	1.90	2.40	72.11	1.46	12.25	1.96	32.04

CONCLUSION.

The results which have been collected and discussed in this and previous reports have shown the wide extent of the variations which occur in the physical and chemical properties of our cereal grains. They have extended over but a few years, and with conditions which have not been sufficiently varied or sufficiently under control. They have served to show, however, how many of the modifying causes are in the hands of the farmer or of the experimental stations, and, to a certain extent, the directions in which advance should be made. The co-operation of practical field-work is now necessary, with laboratory examinations of the results. Until this can be accomplished systematically further progress will be slow and uncertain.

www.ingramcontent.com/pod-product-compliance
Lightning Source LLC
Chambersburg PA
CBHW031607110426
42742CB00037B/1319